CHURCHES OF COUNTY DURHAM

COLIN WILKINSON

AMBERLEY

This edition first published 2025

Amberley Publishing
The Hill, Stroud
Gloucestershire GL5 4EP

www.amberley-books.com

British Library Cataloguing in Publication Data.
A catalogue record for this book is available from the British Library.

ISBN 978 1 3981 2018 1 (print)
ISBN 978 1 3981 2019 8 (ebook)

Typesetting by SJmagic DESIGN SERVICES, India.
Printed in Great Britain.

Appointed GPSR EU Representative:
Easy Access System Europe Oü, 16879218
Address: Mustamäe tee 50, 10621, Tallinn, Estonia
Contact Details: gpsr.requests@easproject.com, +358 40 500 3575

Contents

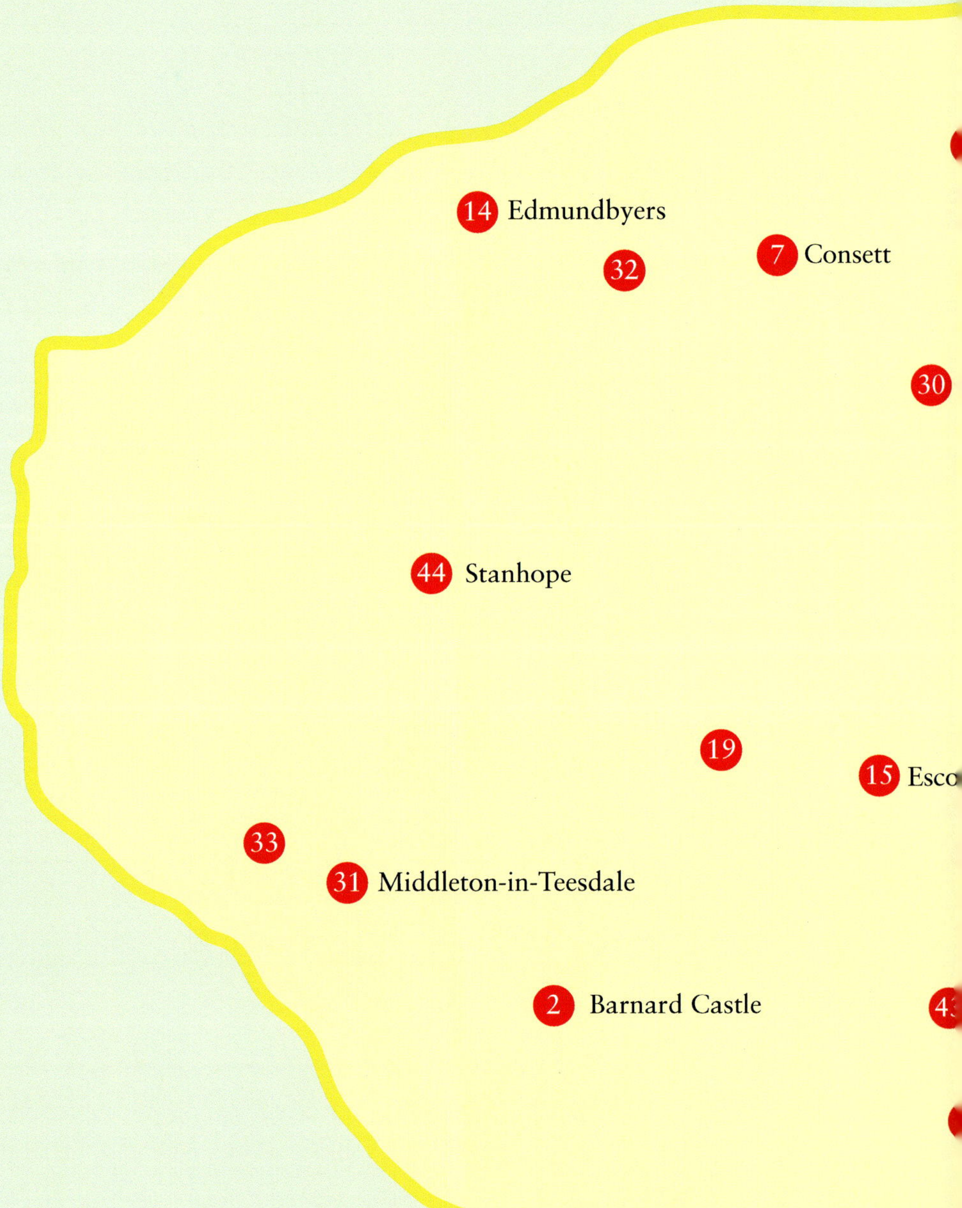
14 Edmundbyers
32
7 Consett
30
44 Stanhope
19
15 Esco
33
31 Middleton-in-Teesdale
2 Barnard Castle
4

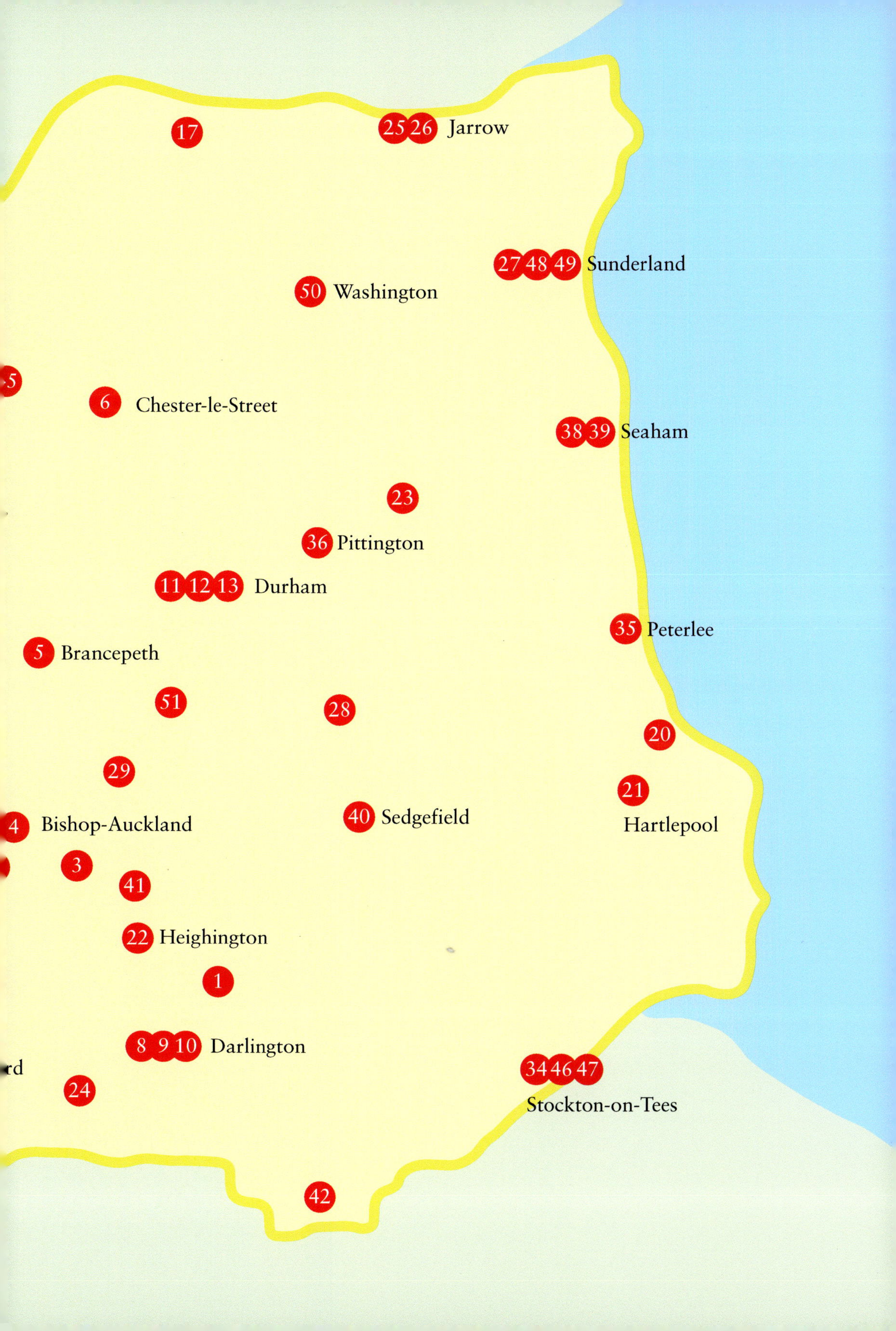
17
25 26 Jarrow
27 48 49 Sunderland
50 Washington
6 Chester-le-Street
38 39 Seaham
23
36 Pittington
11 12 13 Durham
35 Peterlee
5 Brancepeth
51
28
20
29
21
Hartlepool
4 Bishop-Auckland
40 Sedgefield
3
41
22 Heighington
1
8 9 10 Darlington
34 46 47
Stockton-on-Tees
24
42

Key

1. St Andrew, Aycliffe Village
2. St Mary, Barnard Castle
3. St Andrew, South Church, Bishop Auckland
4. Auckland Palace, Bishop Auckland
5. St Brandon, Brancepeth
6. St Mary and St Cuthbert, Chester-le-Street
7. St Mary and Christ Churches, Consett
8. St Andrew, Haughton le Skerne, Darlington
9. St Cuthbert, Darlington
10. Friends Meeting House, Darlington
11. St Cuthbert, Durham
12. St Oswald, Durham
13. Durham Cathedral
14. St Edmund, Edmundbyers
15. St John the Evangelist, Escomb
16. St Mary, Gainford
17. St Mary, Gateshead
18. Gibside Chapel
19. Baptist Church, Hamsterley
20. St Mary Magdalene, Hart
21. St Hilda, Hartlepool
22. St Michael, Heighington
23. Hetton-le-Hole Methodists
24. St Edwin, High Coniscliffe
25. Christ Church, Jarrow
26. St Paul, Jarrow, and 27. St Peter, Monkwearmouth, Sunderland
28. St Helen, Kelloe
29. St John the Evangelist, Kirk Merrington
30. All Saints, Lanchester
31. St Mary the Virgin, Middleton-in-Teesdale
32. All Saints, Muggleswick
33. Methodist Chapel, Newbiggin
34. St Mary, Norton
35. Peter Lee Memorial Church, Peterlee
36. St Laurence, Pittington
37. St Helen, St Helens Auckland
38. St Mary, Seaham
39. St John the Evangelist, Seaham Harbour
40. St Edmund, Sedgefield
41. St John, Shildon
42. All Saints, Sockburn
43. St Mary's, Staindrop
44. St Thomas the Apostle, Stanhope
45. St Andrew, and St Joseph, Stanley
46. Parish Church, Stockton-on-Tees
47. St Mary, Stockton-on-Tees
48. Minster Church of St Michael and All Angels and St Benedict Biscop, Sunderland (formerly St Michael and All Angels)
49. St Andrew, Roker, Sunderland
50. St Boste, Oxclose, Washington
51. Whitworth Church, Whitworth, Spennymoor

INTRODUCTION

This exploration starts in the Dark Ages to find the churches that vie for the position of the oldest in the county, including those that formed part of the monasteries where the Venerable Bede (673–735) worked to produce his histories. However, perhaps the best example from this era, and still standing substantially as built, is the seventh- or eighth-century Saxon church at Escomb.

The Norman invaders follow and to help secure their position in the north the land of the Prince Bishops emerges. Norman masons were busy building churches around the county, as well as the magnificent cathedral and castle on the peninsular, high above the river at Durham. Church building continued through the Middle Ages, adding to the rich heritage of churches to be found in the towns and villages of Durham. Then came a period of turmoil with the Reformation, followed in the seventeenth century by the Civil War and Commonwealth. These centuries saw few new churches. However, by the early years of the eighteenth century new parish churches can be sought out. Also starting to build were other sects, usually on a much simpler scale, as will be seen at the Baptist chapel in Hamsterley and in the early Methodist churches.

The nineteenth century brings a period of dramatic development to the county. Coal had been mined for centuries but demand was increasing as the country's industrial base grew, which prompted new mines to be sunk throughout the Durham coalfield. The availability of work attracted people and the population of County Durham grew from around 150,000 at the start of the century towards 1.2 million. Towns were expanded and new villages emerged. The churches that had been built to serve the manors and agricultural communities were not going to be adequate or in the right place. The established church needed to react to this dramatic growth, but it also faced other challenges. Methodists were often taking the lead in providing places of worship in the developing communities. Catholic emancipation was completed allowing churches to be built. The Church of England authorities did not react well; locally it was realised there was little progress in supplying adequate ministry for the increasing numbers. These shortcomings were highlighted in 1855 by a correspondent in the *Durham Chronicle*, who noted the situation at Leadgate, a new town with mining and iron industries and a population of 5,000. It was 4 miles from the church at Lanchester and a curate was holding services in a room belonging to one of the local businesses, but this just illustrated how 'spiritual provision in the district is poor and scanty'. Action was taken, new churches were built and clergy recruited and trained.

In the early decades of the twentieth century the church was strong and continued to be an integral part of the community. After the Second World War and the austerity of the 1950s the next decade saw significant changes in society, and values changed with the growing affluence. Traditional norms of behaviour were questioned; legislation to decriminalise homosexuality, relaxing of divorce laws and legalising abortion reflected this. The recognition of Sunday as a special day was eroded, church congregations dwindled and many churches became redundant. Nevertheless, the twentieth century did see churches built in the new towns and the expanding suburbs – the splendid St Andrew's in Roker is an example. Alternative uses were sought for the surplus churches but some did not survive. One example was St Paul's in Darlington where, in June 1937, Robert Jardine, the then vicar, achieved some notoriety when he disappeared and turned up in France to conduct the wedding ceremony of Edward and Mrs Simpson at the Chateau de Cande, near Tours. He performed the ceremony despite the refusal by the Church of England to sanction the marriage. This church in Darlington was closed in 1972 and its fate sealed when it was badly damaged by fire a year later.

Before the churches are visited and stories of heroes, saints, martyrs, rebels, witches, kings and a pickled parson can begin, there is a need to note that this

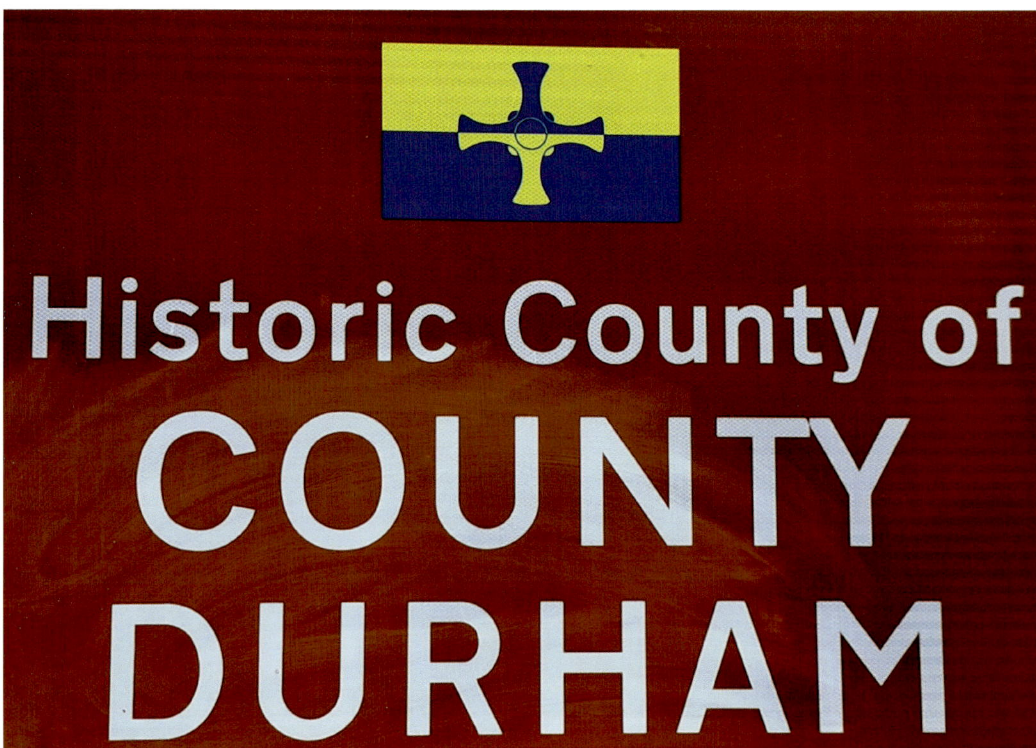

The ancient County of Durham is still signposted.

book travels through the historic county from the Tees to the Tyne from the edge of the Pennine Hills, through the stunning scenery of Teesdale and Weardale towards the glorious coastline.

1. St Andrew, Aycliffe Village

Hidden away from the main village is this fascinating church, with a heritage dating as far back as the eighth century when a church dedicated to St Acca, the Bishop of Hexham between 709 and 732, stood in the settlement. It was the venue for two synods that brought bishops and priests together in 782 and again in 789. Like so many churches it has been enlarged, renovated, and renewed over the centuries but there are reminders of its history and Saxon heritage everywhere. The walls of the Saxon church are incorporated into the arches of the aisles, and the straight joint which marks the end of the Saxon church, and the start of the next building phase, can be seen when looking up from the north aisle. Inside the church are stone carvings from the early times and two decorated crosses, one depicting the crucifixion of St Peter. A simple stone font is thought to be Norman, while in the nave the pews are from the later Jacobean era.

The nineteenth century brought an extensive renovation that involved a new roof and removal of plaster and whitewash from the walls, which revealed the original stonework and uncovered Norman windows. Three new stained-glass

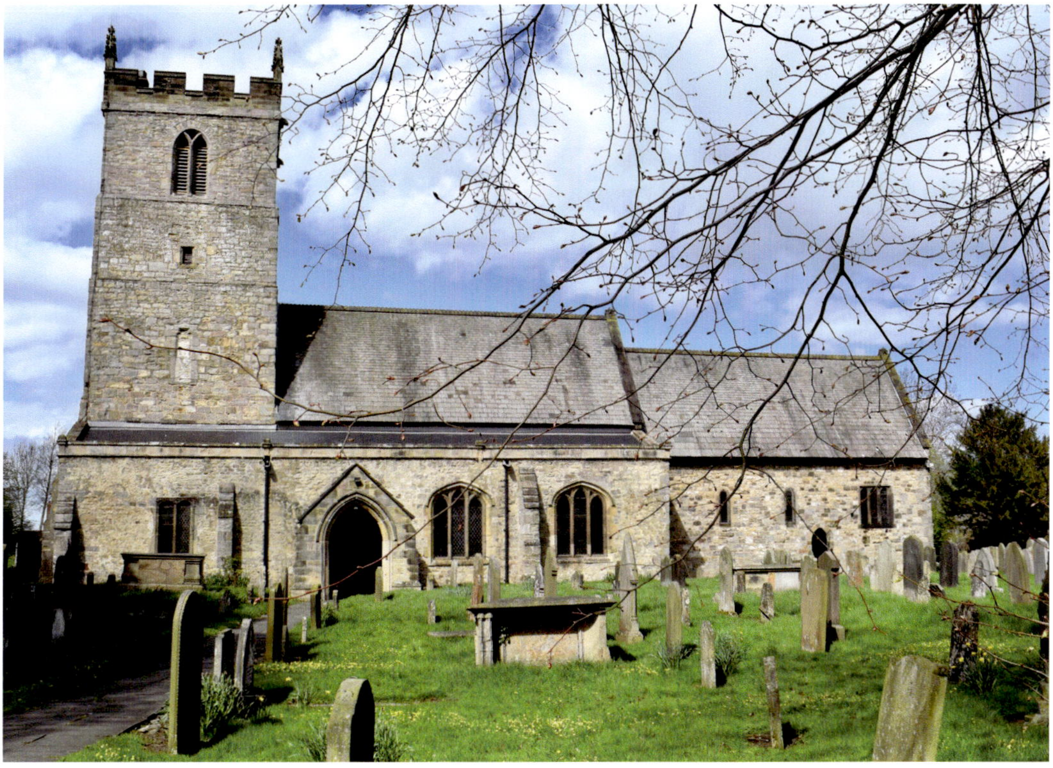

St Andrew, Aycliffe village.

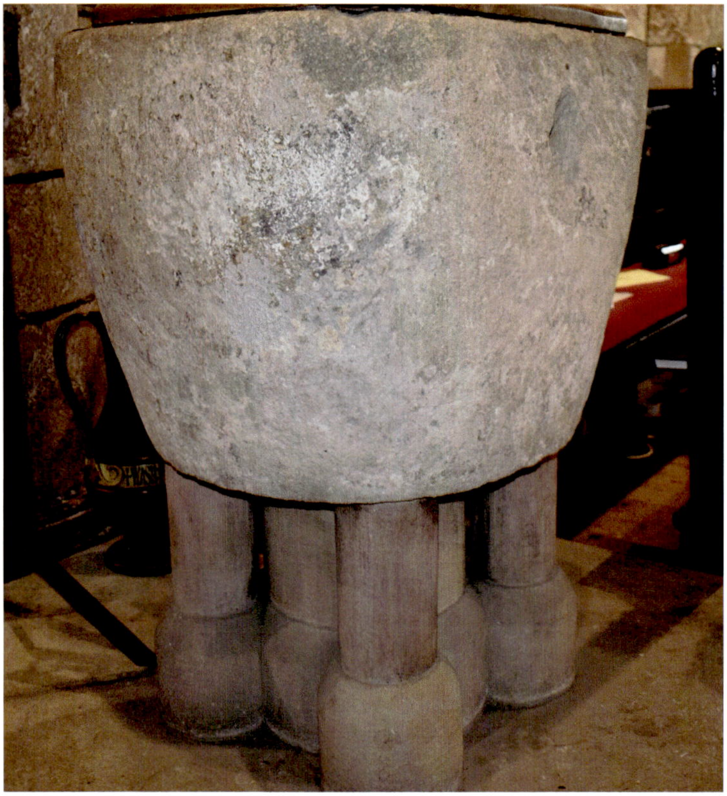

There are many treasures inside St Andrew's at Aycliffe including this font that is thought to be Norman.

windows were added and building work made the tower safe. The Bishop of Durham was at the reopening ceremony in September 1882 and spoke of the fine restoration work; he reflected that this ancient church had been standing longer than the cathedral at Durham.

2. St Mary, Barnard Castle

To secure their position in the north, and to counter any threat of rebellion, the Norman monarchs awarded land to their supporters. In 1095 William II gave Barnard Castle to Guy de Balliol, a knight from Normandy. He was succeeded by Hugh Balliol, who was the man responsible for developing the town's castle on the cliffs above the River Tees. At the same time the church was being built near the castle walls. Dating back to 1130, St Mary's Church was originally a simple oblong shape. It has been extended over the centuries with aisles, a transept and a tower added to produce the grand building standing near the town's octagonal market cross. By the fifteenth century the estate was in the hands of Richard of Gloucester, who would become Richard III. He had funds ready to enlarge the church with the aim of establishing St Mary's as a significant religious centre. His death at Bosworth Fields in 1485 saw the end of these plans.

In 1849 a black flag was flying above the church when the town was struck by an outbreak of cholera. By the start of the nineteenth century a manufacturing

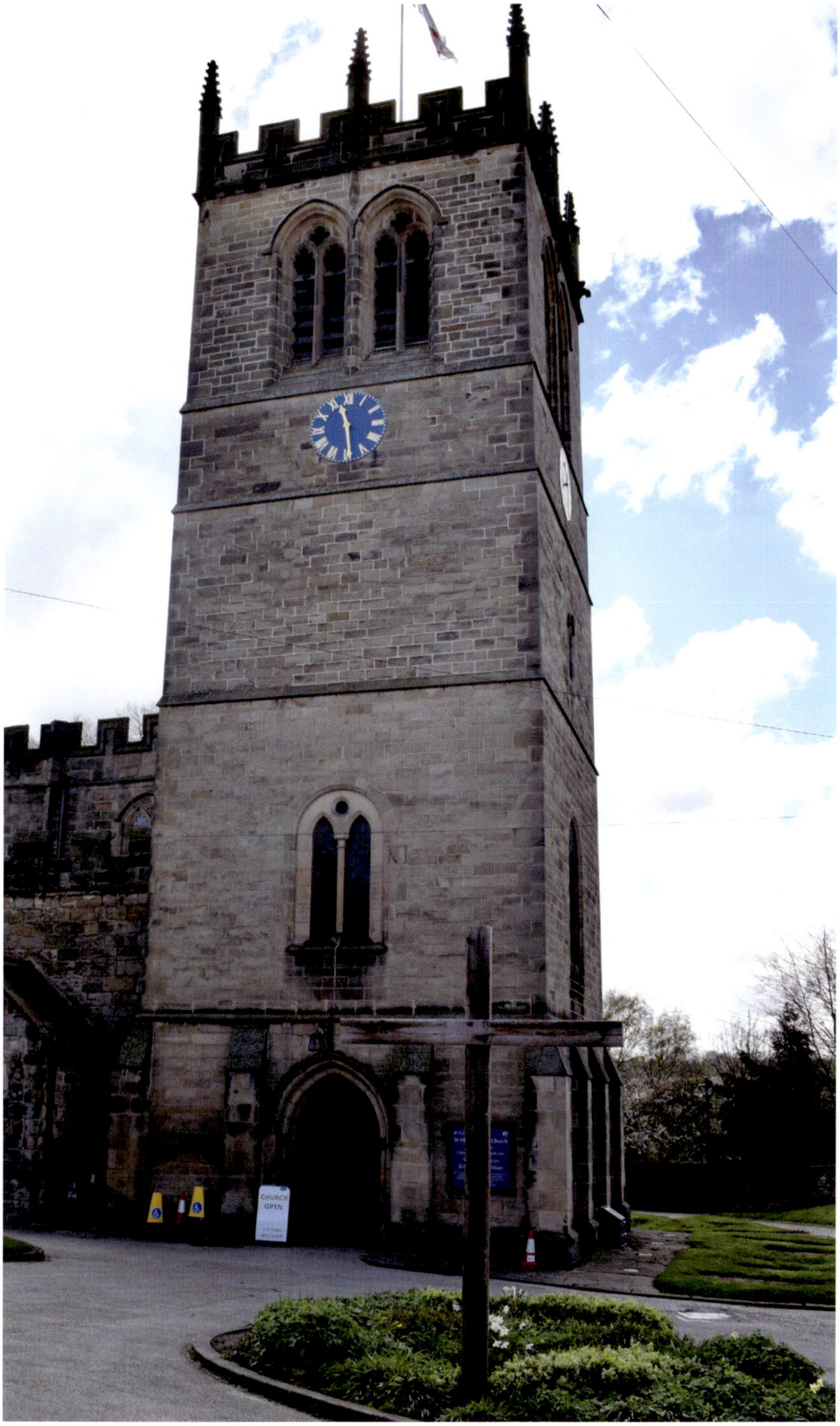

St Mary, Barnard Castle.

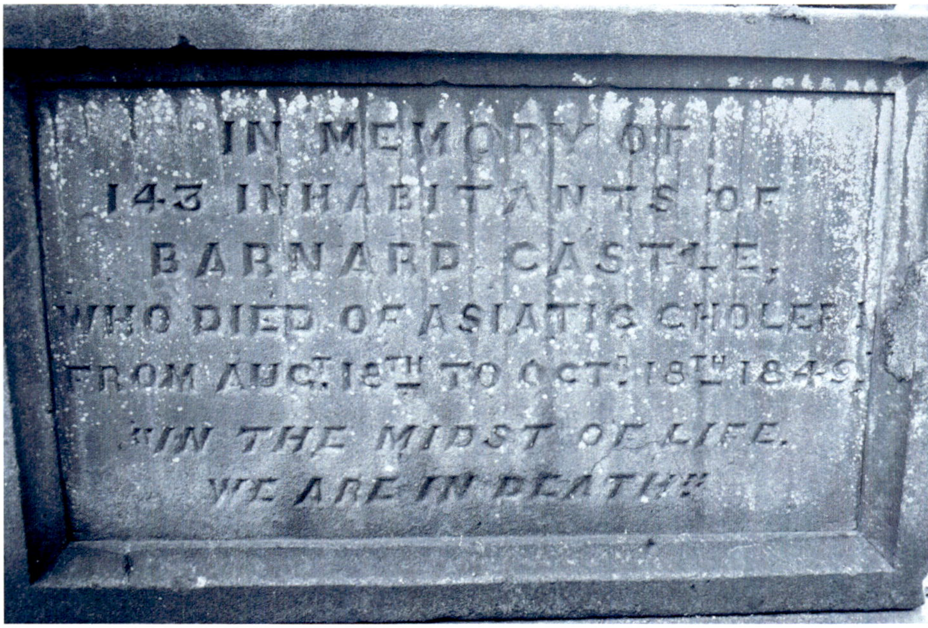

In St Mary's churchyard is the memorial to those who died during the cholera outbreak in 1849.

base had been set up in the town, which included carpet manufacturers and a business that was using the flowing waters of the River Tees to power machinery twisting everything from shoelaces to rope. Work attracted people into the town and the population grew from around 3,000 in 1801 to over 4,500 by 1841. New accommodation was needed but it was not always built to a high standard and housing was soon congregated into narrow yards with little ventilation or natural light. The drainage was described as imperfect, which was an understatement, with main sewers no more than surface drains and in some streets non-existent. When cholera struck, these poor conditions allowed infection to spread. Mr John Pratt, the owner of a carpet mill, was struck down by a violent attack of the disease and died within a day of first feeling ill. His daughter, fourteen-year-old Catherine, followed him a few hours later. A total of 143 people died, and visitors kept away from the 'plague town'. During this time, the vicar was busy, helping those he could and running a soup kitchen. However, the church was not without blame; it is at the top of a bank and the graveyard was not adequately contained. Liquids from decomposing bodies seeped from the burial ground high above the Tees and ran down the bank towards the river, along the way poisoning the wells from which water was drawn.

3. St Andrew, South Church, Bishop Auckland

This church is one of the largest parish churches in the county, no doubt thanks to the canons who were based at the church. In the late eleventh century, builders started working to provide a church for the priests who were excluded from Durham Cathedral when Bishop William de St Calais converted it to a Benedictine monastery. Those clergy who were not Benedictine monks had to leave and were gathered into colleges and collegiate churches were founded for them. They were often referred to as canons as their work was organised around the canons or church regulations, with a dean appointed to oversee their work. Unlike the monks they could hold property and were given land to provide an income. They were also part of the community, not isolated in a cloistered life. Early collegiate churches were also established elsewhere in the county; Darlington, and Norton (near Stockton on Tees) are other examples. In the thirteenth century the canons were able to have the church rebuilt at St. Andrews. They had accommodation in

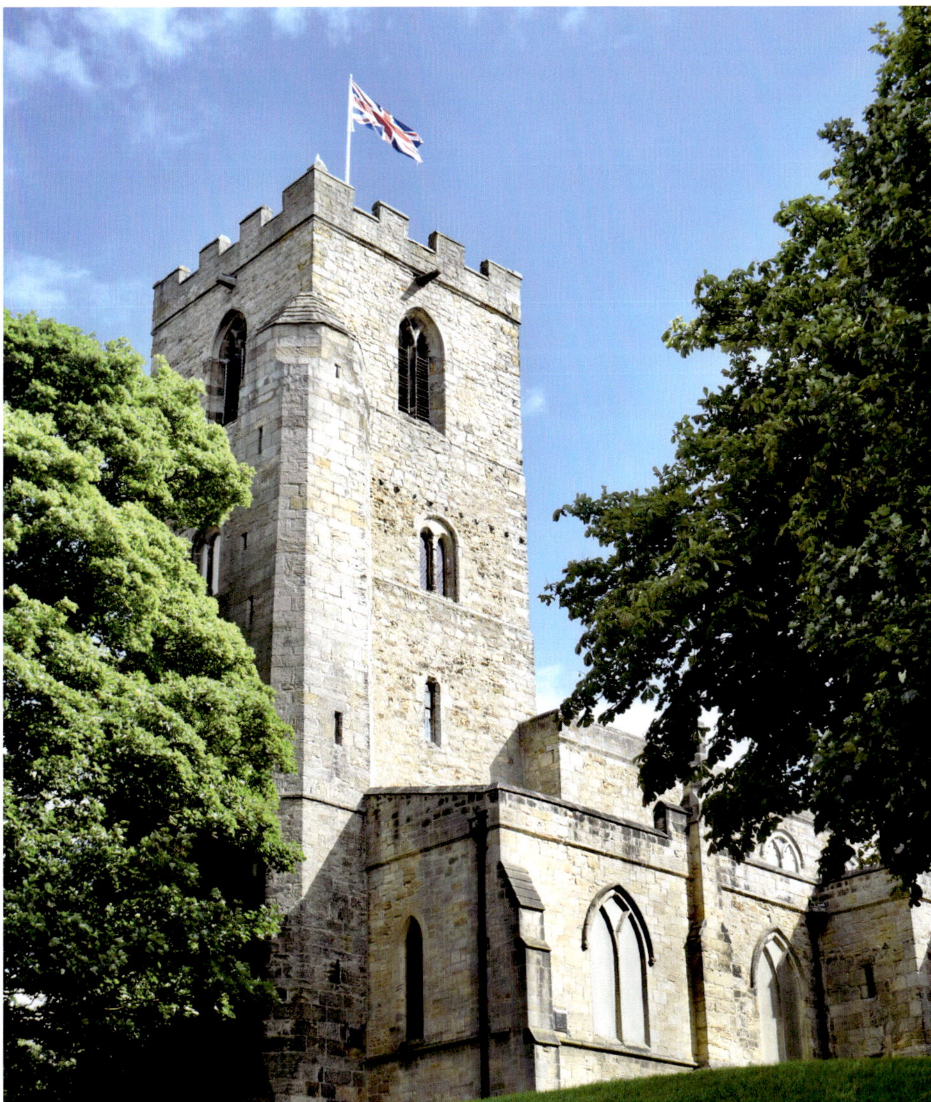

St Andrew South Church, Bishop Auckland.

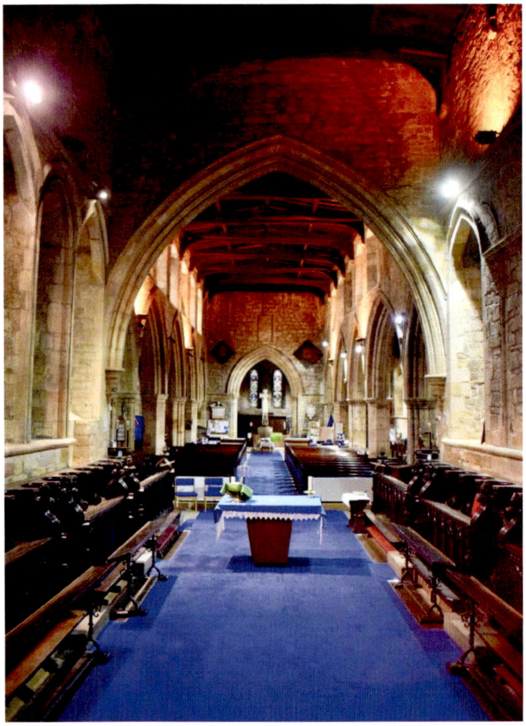

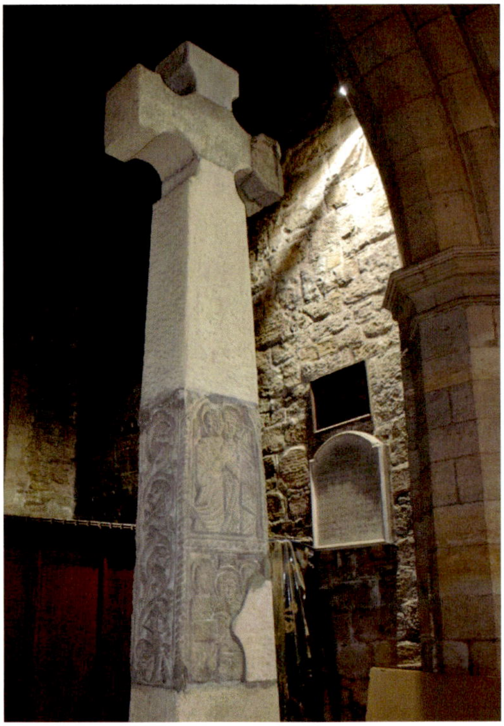

Above left: St Andrew South Church, from the chancel looking towards the nave.

Above right: This rebuilt cross inside St Andrew's South Church incorporates sections of a ninth-century cross.

housing close to the church. It was located over the Deanery Bridge, which crosses the River Gaunless. Some of this housing has survived.

Inside the church, there is much evidence of its long tradition as a religious site. In the west end of the nave is a cross dating to the ninth century that has been rebuilt from the sections that were found underneath the church when restoration work was being undertaken. An effigy of a knight with a boar at his feet brings us to the legend of the Pollard Bear. This wild beast terrorised the folk of Bishop Auckland until a knight, Richard Pollard, rode to the rescue, slayed it, and collected a reward that had been offered by the bishop. There are stalls from the fifteenth century with misericords, or shelves, on the underside of the seat. When the seats were raised, they provided support to those who were required to stand during long services.

4. Auckland Palace, Bishop Auckland

The Durham bishops had a number of grand manor houses built around the county including in Darlington and Stockton. In Darlington, the Bishop's Palace was built near to the parish church of St Cuthbert and survived until it was demolished in the nineteenth century. In Stockton, the manor house was

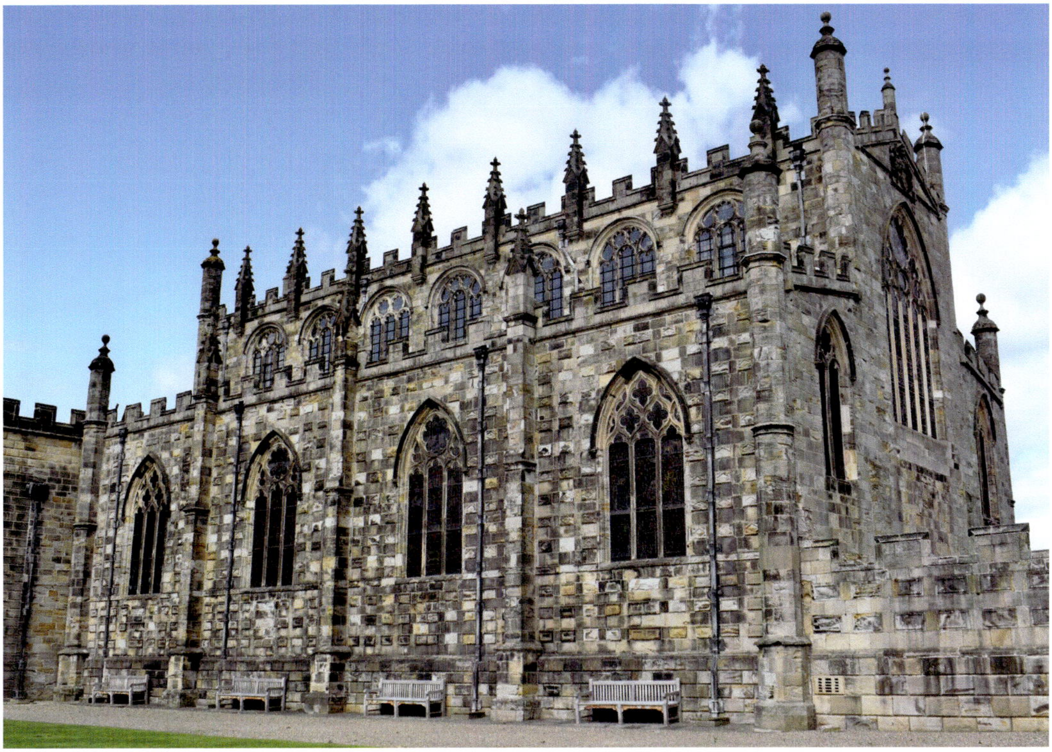

Above: The chapel at Auckland Palace rebuilt by Bishop Cosin in the seventeenth century.

Below: The deer house in the parkland of Auckland Castle.

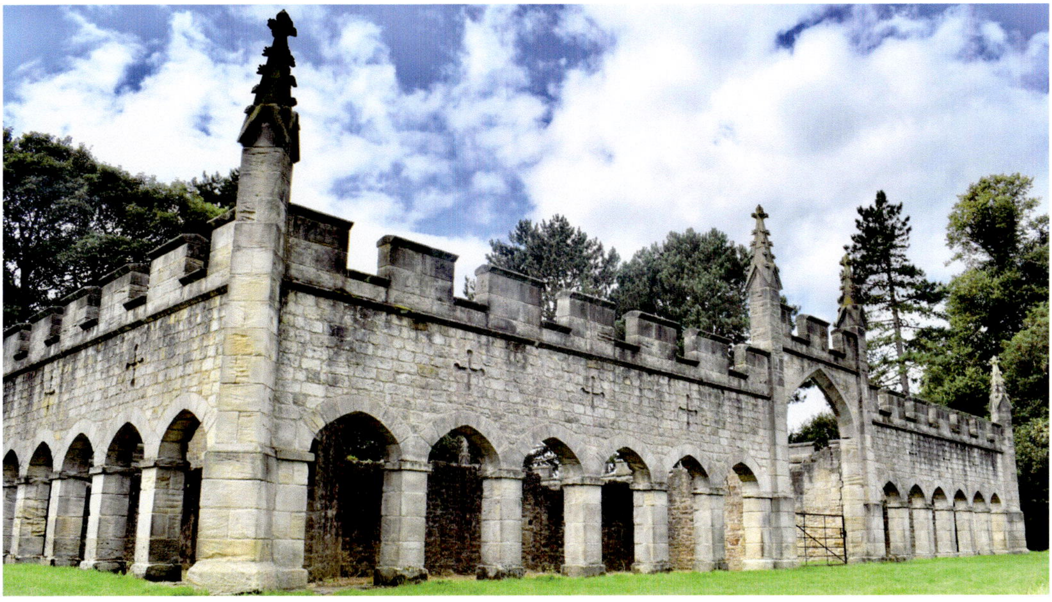

developed to provide accommodation for distinguished visitors, including King John, on visits to the north. Scottish invaders ransacked and burned the house, the rebuilding introduced defences against future attacks, and it became known as Stockton Castle. During the Civil War, the castle was for a time a Royalist stronghold and to ensure this could not happen again its fate was sealed in 1647 when Parliament authorised its destruction.

At Bishop Auckland much of this building, which started as a manor house with a grand hall for Bishop de Puiset, has survived. Started in the late twelfth century, the site continued to be developed by many of his successors to become, after Durham, the bishops' favoured residence. Anthony Bek, who was Bishop of Durham between 1284 and 1310, wanted to improve accommodation close to his hunting grounds and added more buildings and a chapel. During the Civil War and Commonwealth, the chapel was destroyed, but, after the Restoration, Bishop Cosin had the banqueting hall converted into a chapel. John Cosin had been chaplain to Charles I and this association left him taking flight to Europe. However, he returned to become the new Bishop of Durham in 1660 and started restoring the damaged and neglected cathedral and churches. Examples of the woodwork he had installed are still found in the county's churches.

In 1832 the palace became the official residence of the Durham bishops until 2012 when it was transferred to a trust. It is now a visitor attraction. Nearby is the Deer House, built in 1767 by Bishop Richard Trevor. Its purpose was to provide shelter and a feeding place within the palace's parkland.

5. St Brandon, Brancepeth

The church dates from the eleventh century with work continuing, including the extension of aisles and transepts, during the fourteenth century. The tower was gradually given additional stages during the thirteenth and fourteenth centuries. Disaster struck in 1998 when a fire caused catastrophic damage and the interior was destroyed including much of the seventeenth-century woodwork introduced by Bishop John Cosin. However, the extensive rebuilding has produced a wonderfully bright church with light flooding in through the magnificent stained-glass eastern window, installed in 2014.

In November 1569, the bells in churches on the Earl of Westmorland's land, which included St Brandon's Church, are said to have been rung backwards to herald the start of the Northern Rebellion. Close by the church is Brancepeth Castle, which belonged to Charles Neville, Earl of Westmorland, who with Thomas Percy, Earl of Northumberland, led this action against Elizabeth I. These two Catholics had many grievances against the Protestant Elizabeth, who they felt was undermining their position and status. Elizabeth's predecessor, Mary, had restored the Catholic faith and had returned lands that had been taken after a Percy was executed for his part in the Pilgrimage of Grace – the uprising against Henry VIII's closure of monasteries. Elizabeth was guarded against plots to restore the Pope's authority and Catholics were seen as potential traitors. She acted to reduce Northumberland's influence; prestigious roles were taken away including the stewardship of the royal estates. In 1566 copper deposits were found on his land and the queen took the rights to these. Neville had trouble with the Protestant Bishop of Durham who refused to pay the wayleaves for transporting coal across his land. They were not alone and with others their discontent festered. The two saw an opportunity to put right some of the injustice when Mary Queen of Scots fled south from Scotland after she had been implicated in the murder of her husband, Lord Darnley. Mary hoped Elizabeth

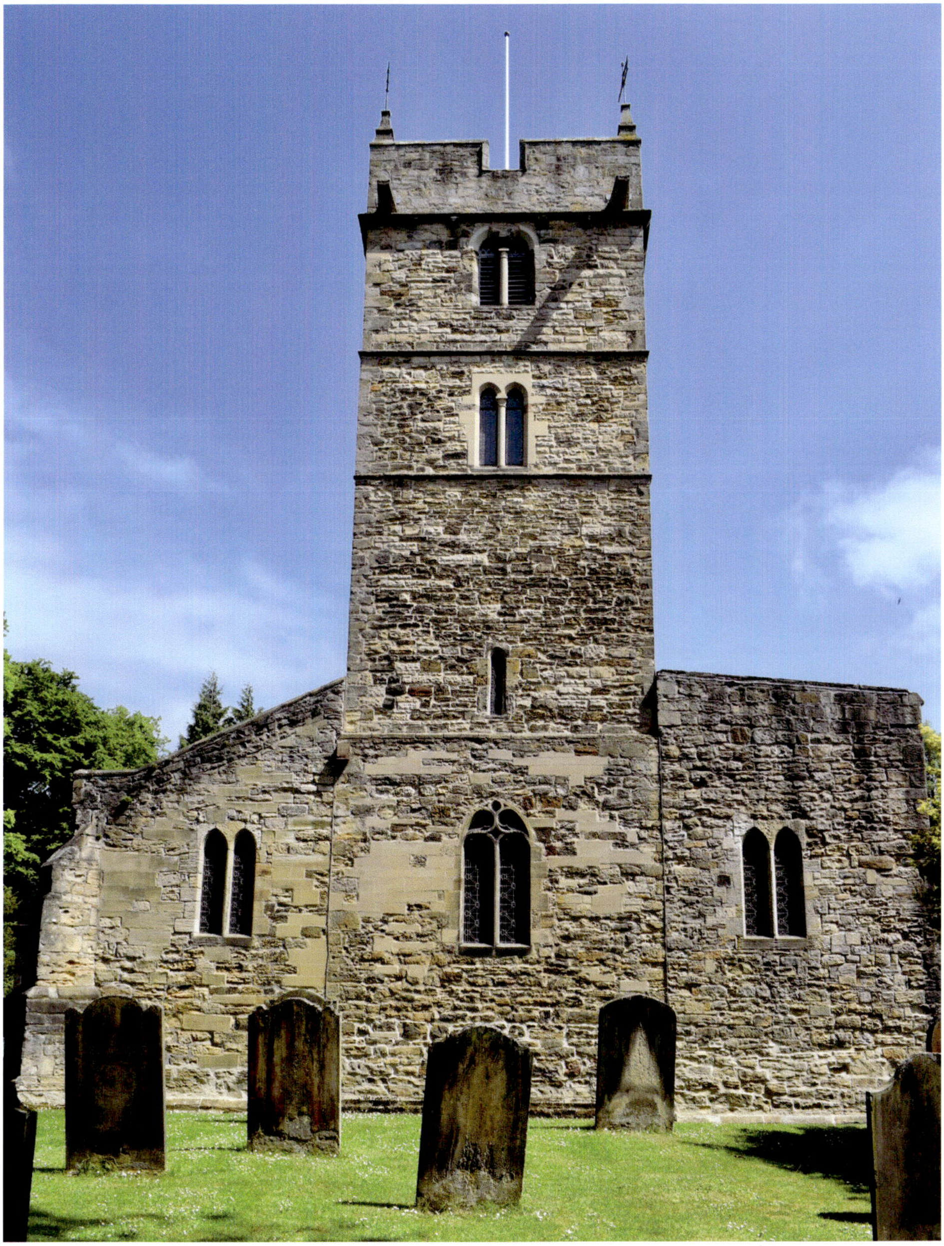

St Brandon, Brancepeth.

would help her reclaim the Scottish throne; however, Elizabeth was wary of Mary and her Catholicism. Mary posed a threat to her position as some argued that she had a better claim to the throne than Elizabeth, who was the daughter of Anne Boleyn. Anne's marriage to Henry VIII could be viewed as illegal, making Elizabeth illegitimate. On the other hand, Mary's lineage could not be questioned as she was the granddaughter of Henry VIII's sister, Margaret Tudor. Elizabeth had Mary held in Bolton Castle in Wensleydale. A web of plots grew around Mary, aimed at giving her the English throne and to return the authority of the Pope. The northern earls hatched their own plan to replace Elizabeth with Mary. Elizabeth's aide in the north heard of the plot and naturally informed the queen, who demanded that the two earls present themselves in London. Knowing what their fate would be, they decided they were left with no alternative but to act; they called their supporters together and on 14 November 1569 entered Durham and held a Catholic mass in the cathedral.

The rebels moved south, recruiting supporters as they went. Hartlepool was taken in the hope that the Spanish would send a force to support them if they had a safe harbour available. They also turned on Barnard Castle, surrounded

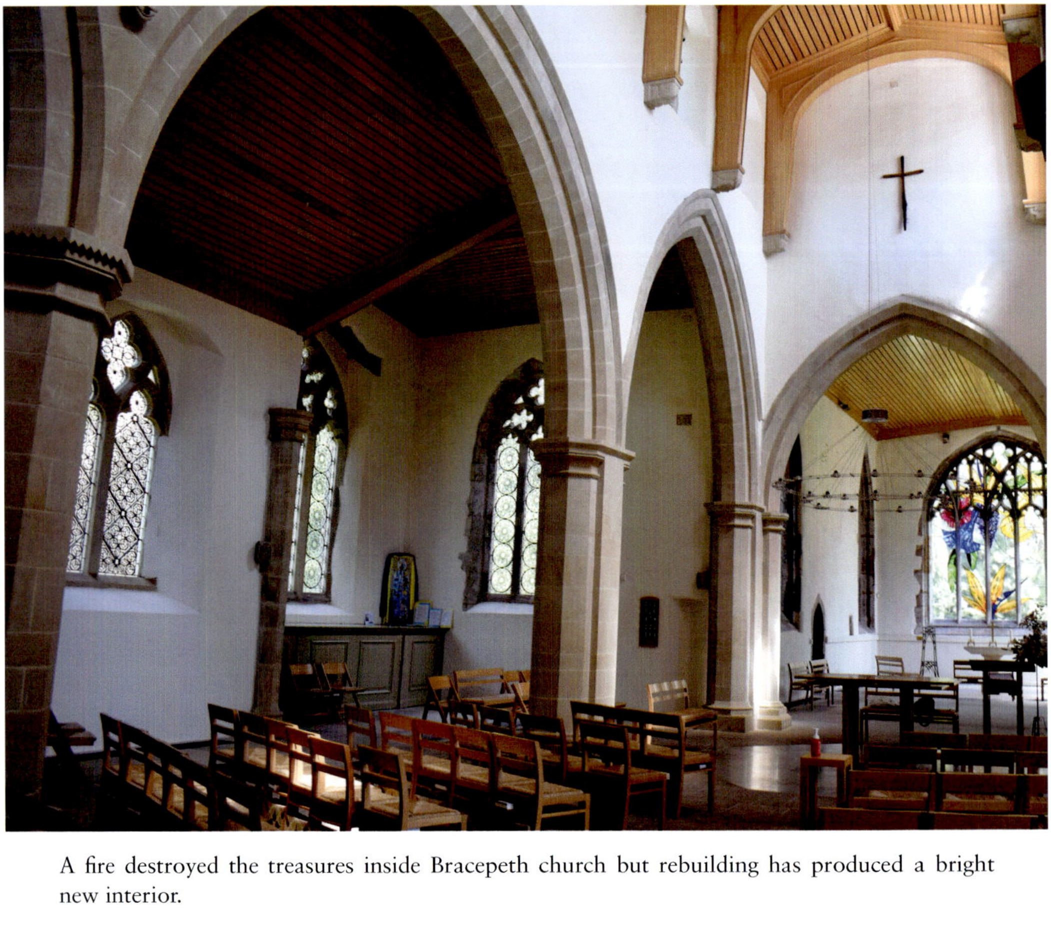

A fire destroyed the treasures inside Bracepeth church but rebuilding has produced a bright new interior.

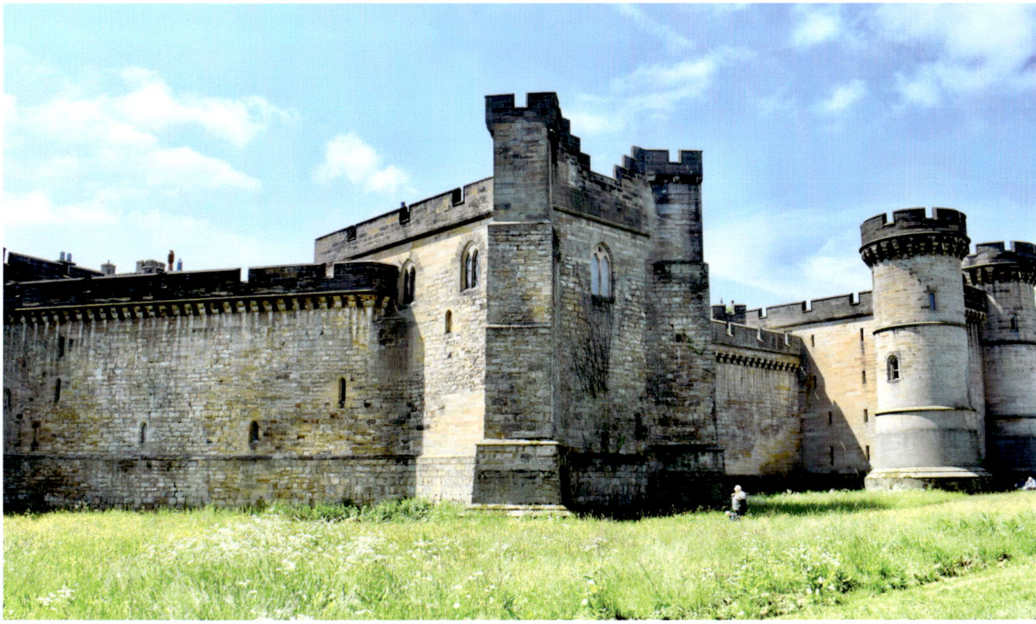

Brancepeth Castle near to St Brandon's Church.

the castle, which had within the walls 700–800 men brought together by George Bowes. The insurgent force triumphed; they breached the castle walls and many of the Bowes soldiers joined rebel cause. Bowes capitulated and was allowed to leave the town; he went to York and joined the Protestant stronghold there. This success was short lived. Troops arrived from the south by mid-December and were joined by men from York. Then the queen's ships arrived in Hartlepool. The earls fled and it was the ordinary folk who had taken part that were singled out for retribution. George Bowes was given the job, and after his defeat at Barnard Castle, he was ready to take revenge as he travelled around the county hanging the guilty. The Earl of Northumberland was caught in Scotland and returned to England to be executed. Westmorland escaped to the continent.

6. St Mary and St Cuthbert, Chester-le-Street

St Cuthbert has strong links with Chester-le-Street. He was born around 635, and at the age of seventeen chose a life dedicated to the church. He entered the monastery at Melrose, then, after a time at Ripon, moved to Lindisfarne. After ten years of missionary work Cuthbert chose life as a hermit and left Lindisfarne for a hermitage on Inner Farne. Later he gave up the reclusive life to be appointed Bishop of Lindisfarne. Sometime around 687 he died. His body was enshrined at Lindisfarne, he was declared a saint, and the island became a site of pilgrimage. Donations of money and valuable objects flowed into the monastery and provided the finance to allow monks to be employed to produce the magnificent Lindisfarne gospels.

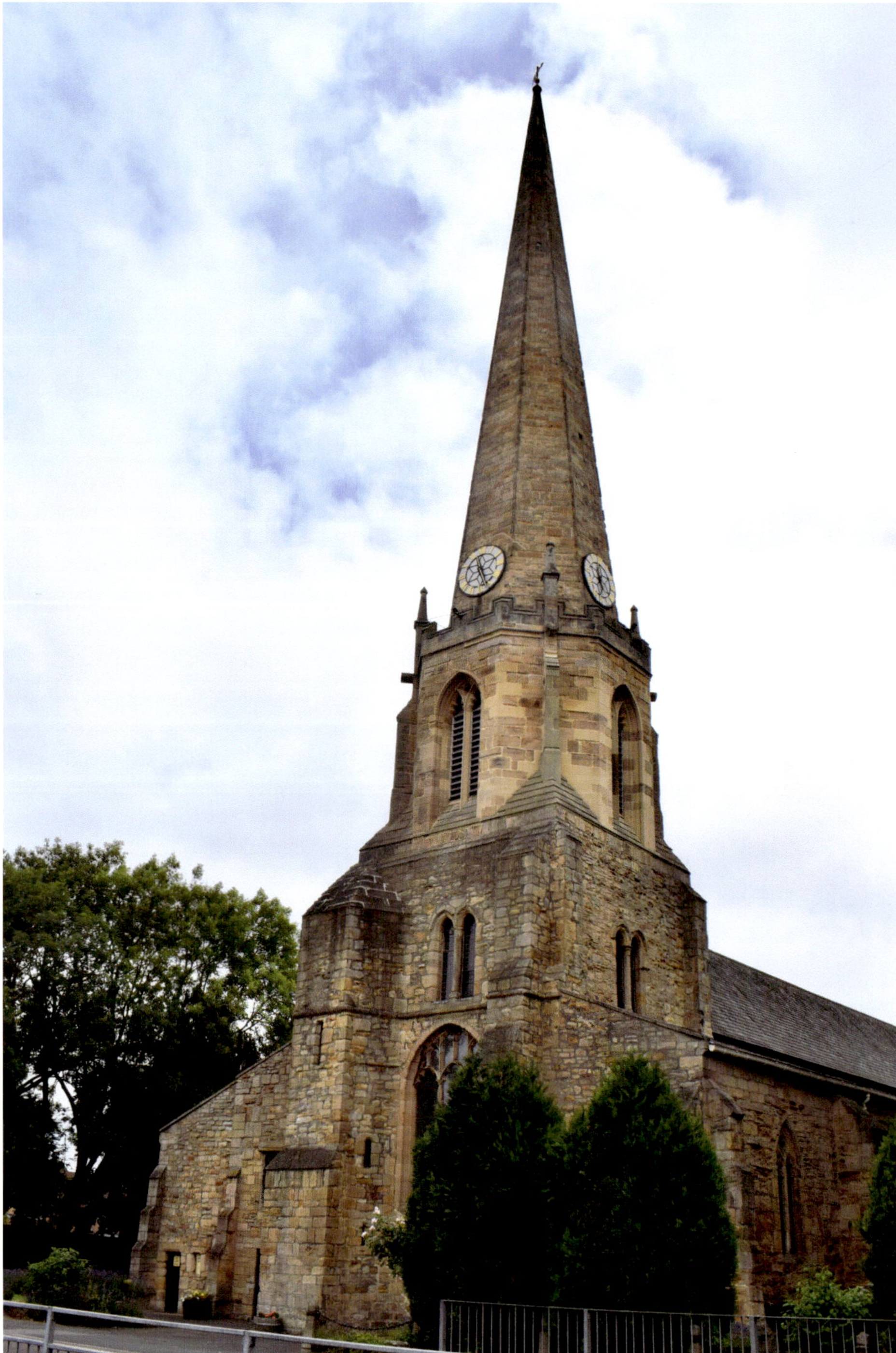

St Mary and St Cuthbert, Chester-le-Street.

The peace at Lindisfarne was disturbed by Viking raiders, who looted and damaged the monastery in the late eighth century. During the next century the raids continued, and the monks were left with little choice but to leave. They fled, taking the body of Cuthbert and the remaining treasures with them. They settled in Chester-le-Street where the Northumbrian king gave them the old Roman fort in the town for a base, together with extensive lands to provide an income. In 934 Athelstan, who had become the king of much of the south of the country, and then took Wales and Northumbria to become regarded as the first King of the English, visited Chester-le-Street on his way to take Scotland. He prayed for strength and wrapped the body of St Cuthbert in an embroidered cloak, the remains of which are displayed in Durham Cathedral.

Concerned about the Viking invaders moving further inland, the monks set off again, reaching Ripon before turning north. The story is told that wherever the monks rested with the remains of Cuthbert a church dedicated to him was founded. There are certainly many churches recognising Cuthbert in the county but perhaps this is little more than a story as it is only to be expected that this northern saint has been celebrated in the region. Eventually the monks settled on a high promissory above the River Wear at Durham.

St Mary and St Cuthbert's Church at Chester-le-Street dates from 1056. It was built on the instructions of Bishop Ethelric on the site where a wooden shrine to St Cuthbert had been erected by the monks. Sometime around 1200 work started to expand the church. A fascinating feature from the fourteenth century is the Anchorage, which was occupied by a succession of hermits who spent their life in the small chamber that had been added to the side of the church. One concession to this solitary existence was a narrow opening in the wall that allowed the recluse to see the alter in the church and listen to the services. Later, the anchorage was expanded and given over to accommodating poor widows; even so it is still a very compact building. It is now a museum with reminders of Roman Chester-le-Street and the life of an Anchorite.

7. St Mary and Christ Churches, Consett

Work on St Mary's Church in the Blackhall area of the town started in 1854. Disaster struck in February 1856 when gale force winds destroyed the part-completed work and it took another year for the church to be opened. Helped with funding contributed by the Irish employees at the ironworks, Father Francis Kearney was the driving force that brought this, the first Catholic church, to town. He had been trained at Ushaw College, which had been opened in 1808 to provide education for Catholic priests. Its roots go back to the late eighteenth century and the French Revolution. Pontop Hall, near Dipton, had long been a Catholic stronghold and provided sanctuary for priests who escaped the terrors of the revolution in France. These were English priests who had been training in the college at Douai until the revolutionaries closed it and imprisoned the staff and students. They managed to escape to England – some found their way to County Durham and found refuge at Pontop Hall. The hall was not suited to accommodating so many and a new base was found at Crook Hall (now demolished), while a site for a new prestigious college was found at Ushaw.

From Ushaw, Father Kearney worked at the church at Brooms, Leadgate, and soon had to turn his attention to the ever-expanding Consett. In 1840 The Derwent Iron Company set up its blast furnaces to make use of the local supply of iron ore, coal and limestone. It brought momentous change, transforming Consett from no more than a gathering of farmhouses into a growing town, which in those early days was a wild, unruly place with little policing. Hostility grew between the English workers and the large contingent of Irish people, who had left their homes to escape the hard times that the years of famine, caused by the failure of the potato crop, had brought. This developed into a tense and bitter hatred. In 1847 reports told of fights breaking out between the two groups, with 3,000 taking to the streets and hundreds injured. Disturbances continued; in 1858 there was potential for a major battle when the two groups gathered, armed with what they could find, facing each other across the town ready to do battle. Father Kearney was amongst those urging restraint and managed to prevent fighting in the streets until eventually they dispersed when

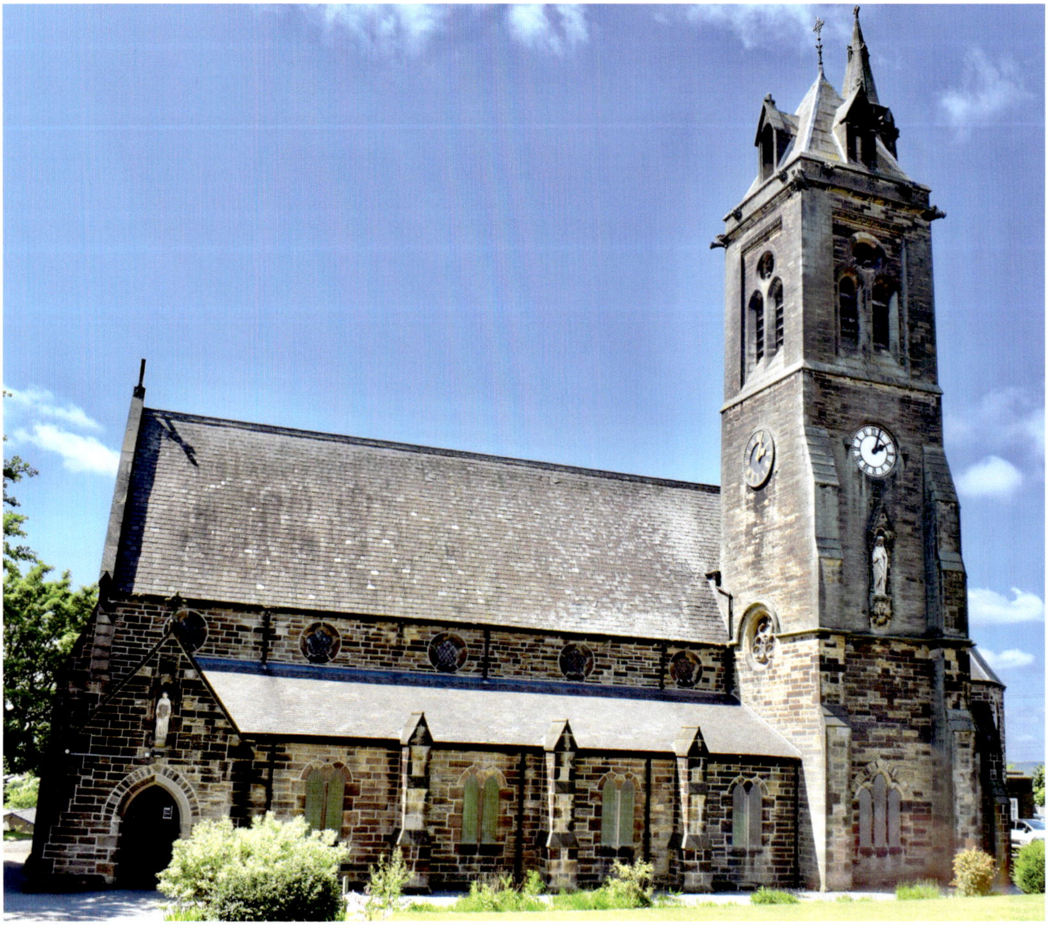

St Mary, Blackhill, Consett.

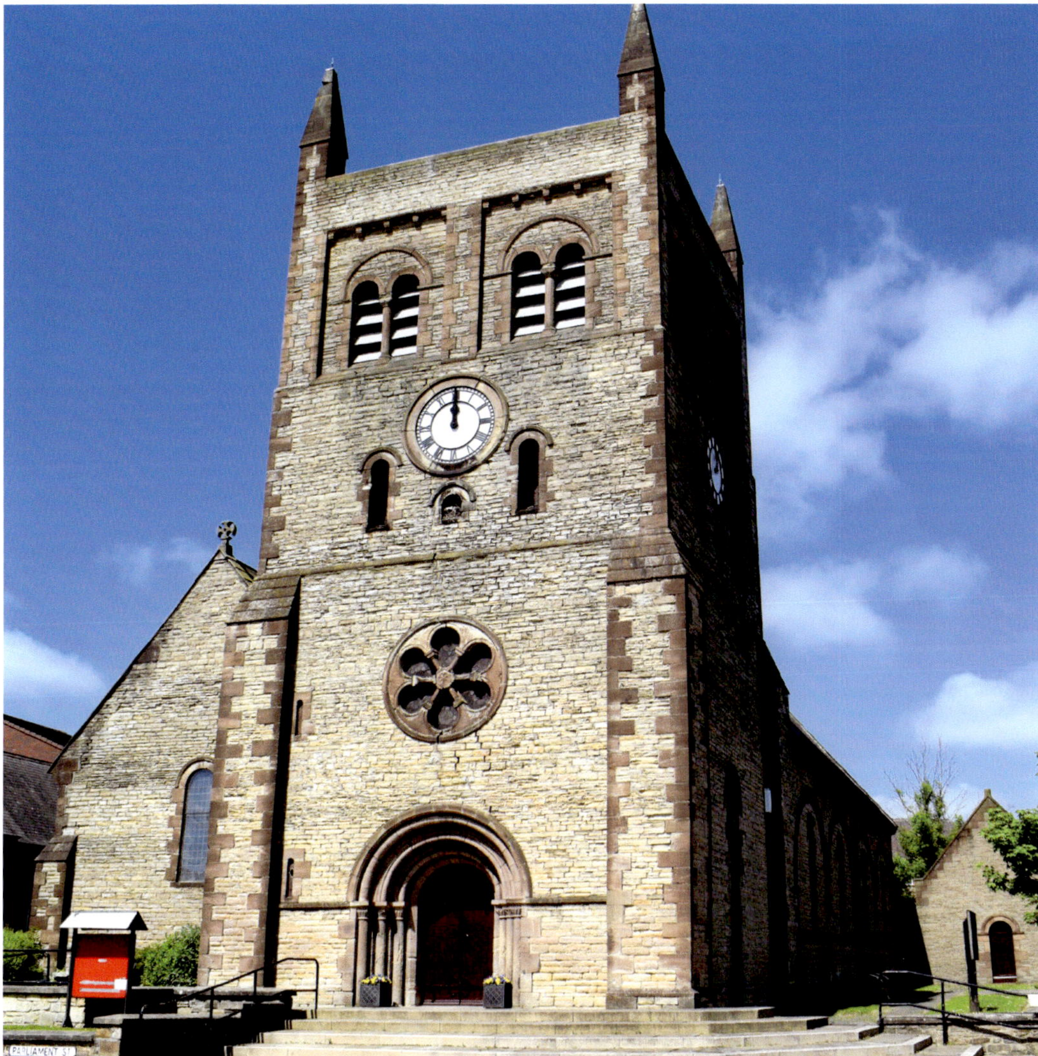

All Saints, Consett.

300 soldiers arrived. Whilst the Catholics were the first to have a church in the town, the Anglican authorities did react and formed a new parish at Consett in 1862 and the new Christ Church opened in 1869.

8. St Andrew, Haughton le Skerne, Darlington

Haughton le Skerne, now a suburb to the east side of Darlington, was once a separate village warranting a mentioned in the Boldon Book. This was the survey ordered by Bishop de Puiset in 1183 to schedule and value the bishop's extensive holdings (County Durham did not appear in the Domesday Book, the survey ordered by William I, as the revenue from lands above the Tees was in the hands

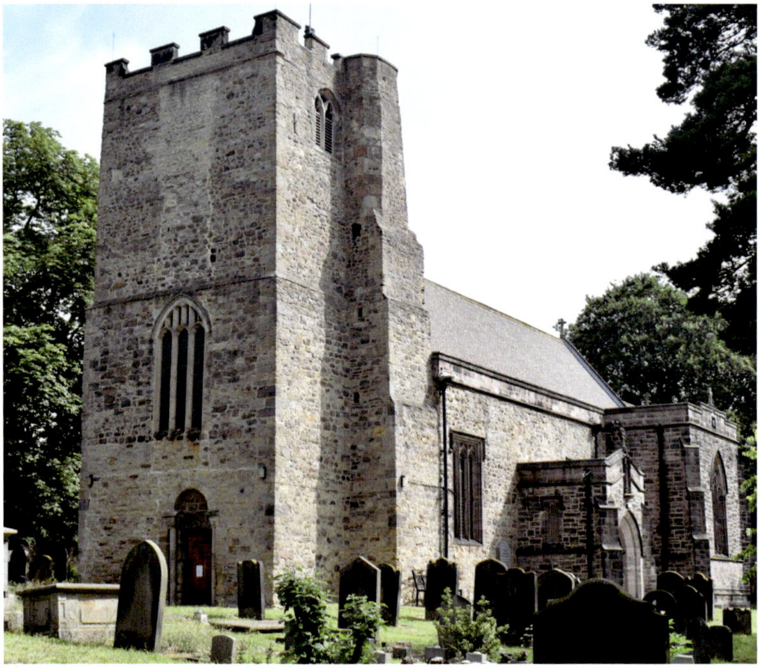

Left: St Andrew, Haughton le Skerne, Darlington, dating from 1125.

Below: Gated pews from the early seventeenth century at St Andrew, Haughton le Skerne.

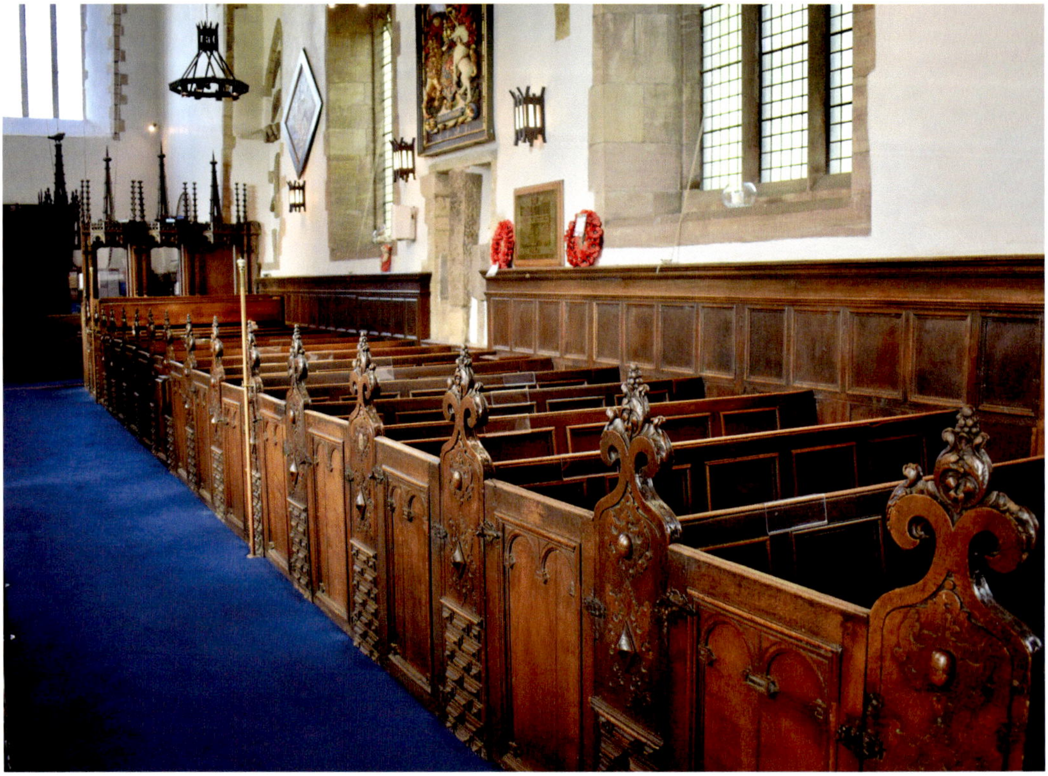

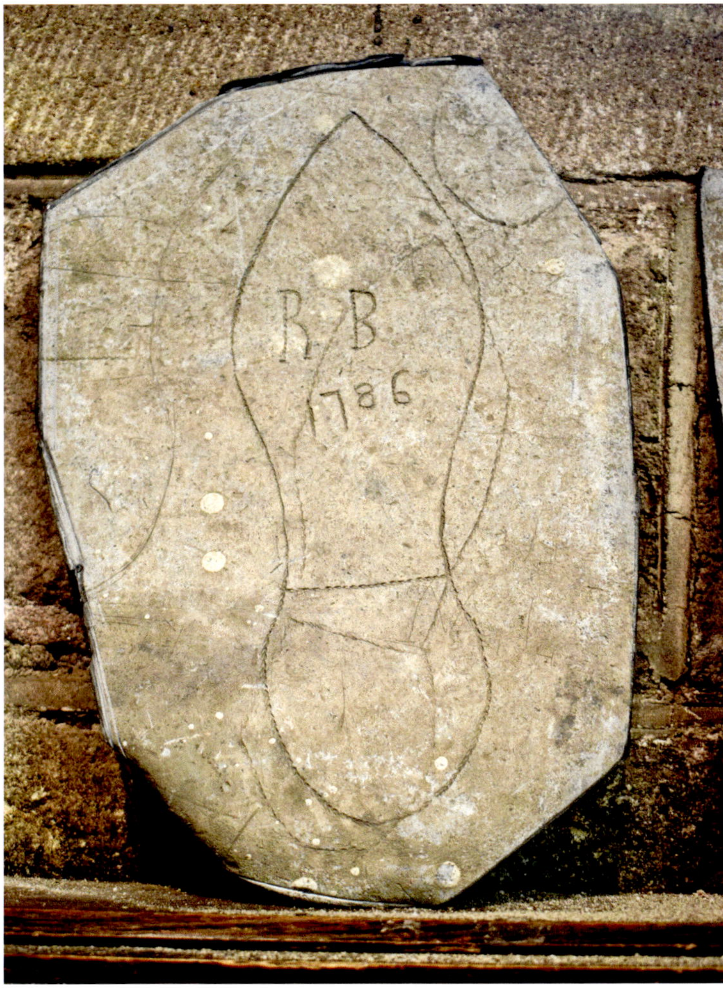

A craftsman working on the roof at St Andrew, Haughton le Skerne, left this reminder.

of the bishops). At Haughton there was Adam, who held the lease on a farm and looked after the bishop's houses in Darlington. The duties of the tenants included working for the bishop two days each week between the feast of St Peter's Chains to the feast of St Martin (August until November).

Building this small Norman church, with a single aisle and short transepts, was started around 1125. The tower was added, in stages, during the thirteenth and fourteenth centuries. Inside there is Saxon stonework suggesting that the church is built on a site that had religious connections from an earlier era. Much of the furniture was produced in the early decades of the seventeenth century; the pews are gated with decorated panels and have their age confirmed by a parishioner who chose to carve 1639 into one. The display of a royal coat of arms became a mandatory requirement after the restitution of Charles II. At Haughton, the plaque recognises George II – probably an earlier panel with lettering revised with the changing monarchs.

9. St Cuthbert, Darlington

During a major restoration of the church by the Victorians, it was reported that foundations of a Saxon church were found, confirming that the site had long religious connections. By the late eleventh century it seems to have become a collegiate church used by the clergy moved from Durham when the cathedral became a monastic site. Hugh de Puiset was Bishop of Durham between 1153 and 1195 and was responsible for having the church rebuilt. This is the church, renovated and adapted over the years, that stands in the town centre today. Bishop de Puiset needed a grand church to complement the Bishop's Palace with its extensive park land he had built a little to the south of the church. The Bishop's Palace was the first place in Durham that the church authorities could accommodate their guests arriving from the south. The palace was used by royal visitors, including in 1502 when Margaret Tudor, the daughter of Henry VII, was on her way to marry James IV of Scotland.

Inside the church there are reminders of its long history including remnants of Saxon cross heads found during the renovation work. There are also fifteenth-century chancel stalls and misericords, which feature carvings of monsters and angels, an ancient font and a magnificent seventeenth-century font cover. Font covers were used to stop holy water being stolen. Early covers were simple – just a lid with a padlocked iron bar – but, as seen in Darlington, they became extravagant, decorated statements.

For many years the church housed the town's grammar school. It was given a royal charter in 1563 by Elizabeth I, although it had been founded a few years earlier by Robert Marshall from the nearby village of Cockerton. Initially teaching was undertaken in a corner of St Cuthbert's Church. Later a schoolhouse was built in the grounds of the church. This association of the church with education was not unusual. Through the county several Barrington schools were set up using money given by Shute Barrington, the Bishop of Durham from 1791 to 1826, from the royalties from coal mined on church lands. The school at Bishop Auckland became a flagship Barrington school and was used as a training school for teachers. Sunday schools were run by the church and for some children this was the only chance they had of gaining some education, particularly when they were needed to contribute to the family's income. In 1823 there were children at work in Darlington's textile mills and it was noted 'no less than 1,000 looms are constantly employed here ... [which] occasions daily work for multitudes of dyers, spinners, combers and children who wind the thread and yarn'. The first Sunday school in Darlington seems to have been opened by Reverend Topham at St Cuthbert's Church. An early attempt by the Methodists to run a Sunday school in the town did not last, as poor behaviour on the part of the children attending lead to closure. It does seem the Methodists in Sunderland had a better experience. In 1790 John Wesley reported 'in the morning preached a sermon at Monkwearmouth, for the Sunday school, which had already cleared the streets of all the children that used to play there on Sunday from morning to evening'. The dissenting groups were becoming involved nationally in education. The British and Foreign Society was formed in 1808 to provide schools on a non-denominational basis. Three years

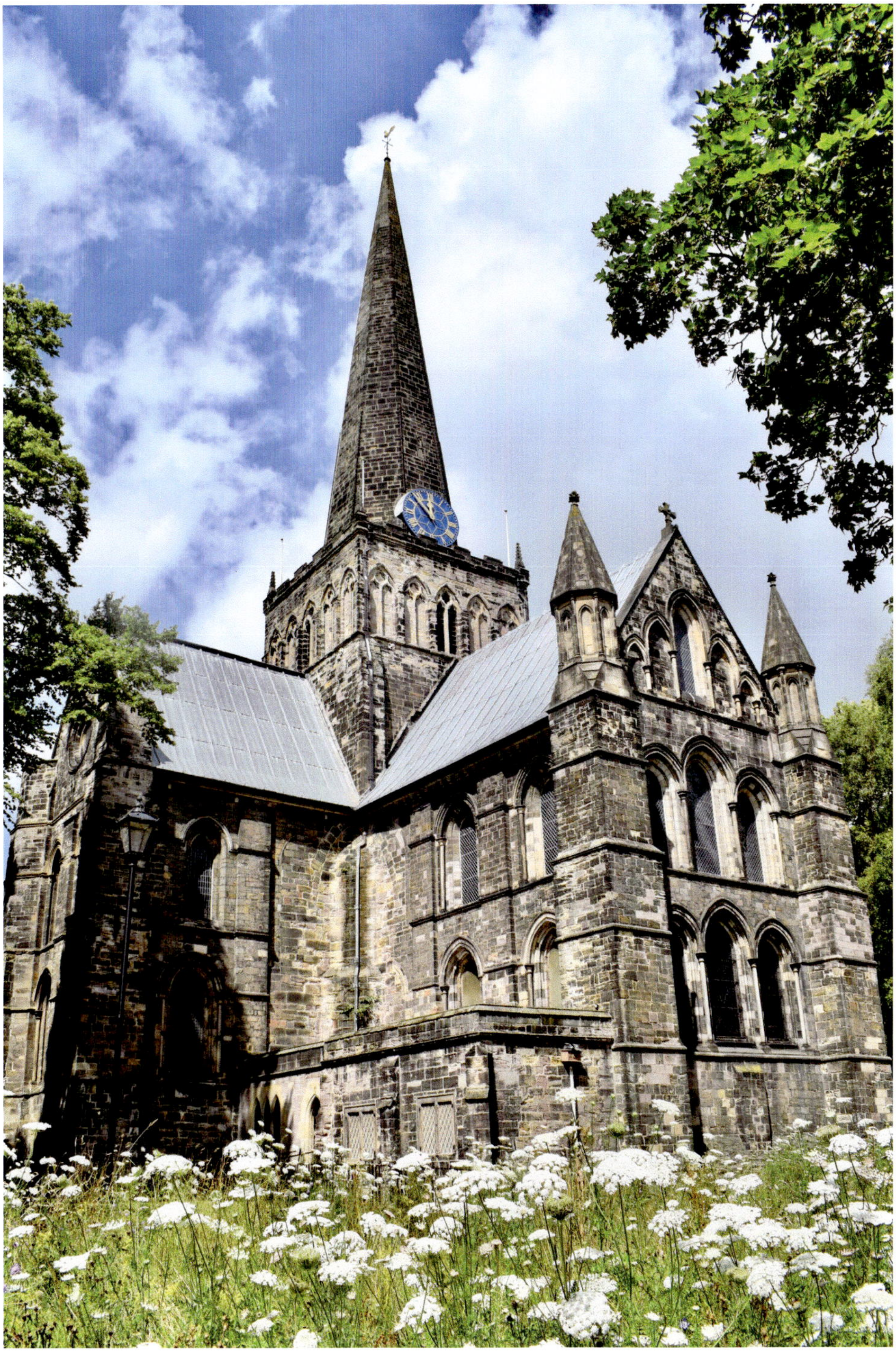

St Cuthbert, Darlington.

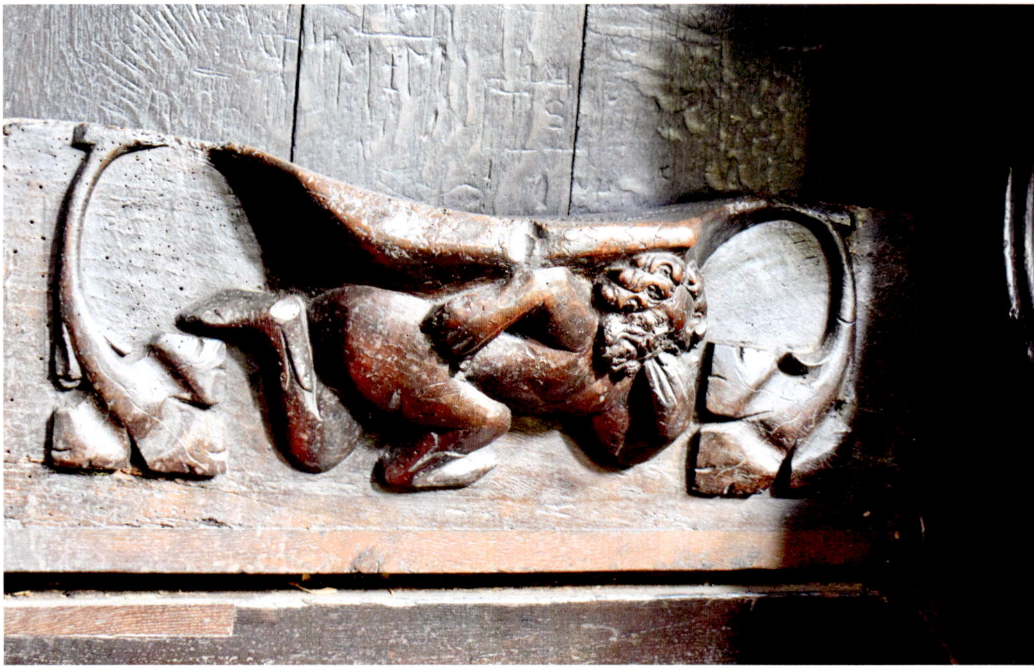

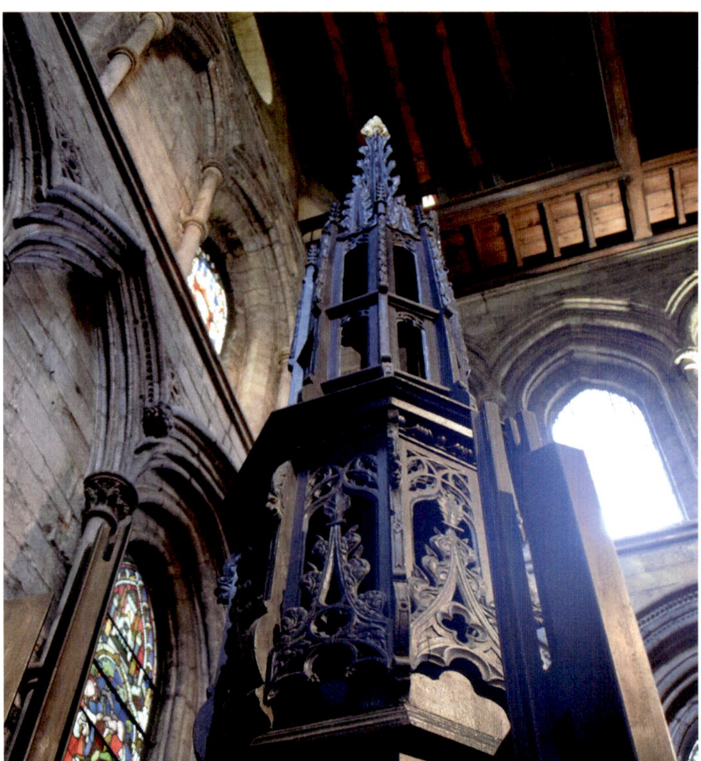

Above: The misericords at St Cuthbert, Darlington. Whoever carved these was having some fun in producing this curious detailing.

Left: The outstanding font cover at St Cuthbert, Darlington.

later, the Church of England authorities reacted, concerned that 'if the great body of the nation be educated in principles other than those of the Established Church, the consequence must be alienation of minds' and formed The National Society for Promoting Education of the Poor on the Principles of the Established Church in England and Wales.

10. Friends Meeting House, Darlington

The Civil War brought considerable disruption to the country. During the years of the Commonwealth a new structure for the national church started to emerge; bishops were removed, churches were made plainer, and the future organisation of the church debated. During this time new sects emerged, the Quakers being one. In the early years they were a radical group, interrupting church services to proclaim their view that true religion was found in the inner light of the spirit. The Quakers explained that people should be influenced by

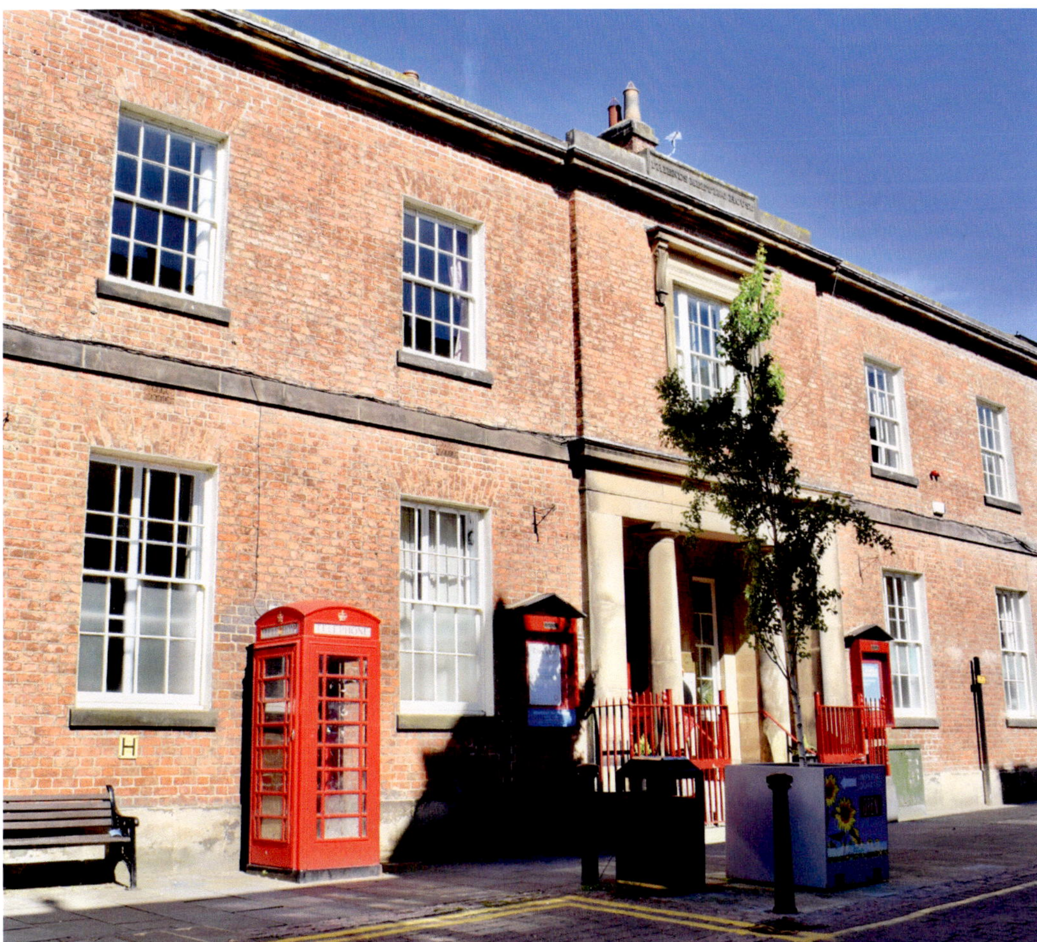

Friends Meeting House, in Skinnergate, Darlington, dating from 1840.

the spirit that was within them and this gave the true voice of God; consequently, there was no need for much of the tradition that had been built up by the church and they therefore saw no need for an organised church. George Fox is often noted as the main founder of the Quakers, but there were other leaders including James Naylor, whose treatment illustrates the concern that the spread of movements that were threatening the Church needed to be checked. In 1656 Naylor was found guilty of blasphemy when he entered Bristol on an ass, as Jesus did into Jerusalem. He was sentenced to be branded, his tongue bored, and then flogged before serving life in prison.

Charles II (r. 1660–85) wanted to show more religious tolerance but he was prevented in this by a parliament wanting to ensure the supremacy of the Anglican Church. The Clarendon Code was a group of legislation introduced in the 1660s to restrict the activities of Nonconformists. Amongst the restrictions was the holding of religious meetings of more than five people outside the Established Church. Darlington Quakers fell afoul of this regulation. Cuthbert Tomlinson was fined £20 for holding a meeting in his house and those attending 10*s*, or for a first offence it was reduced to 5*s*. Whilst the early meetings of Quakers were held in private houses, by 1678 a meeting room was in use; this was on the site of the existing building, which replaced the original around 1840. Without the stonework declaring the building to be the Friends Meeting House, the exterior, which faces the street in the town centre, could be taken for a grand house, not a church. Behind the meeting house is a Quaker cemetery, the resting place for many members of the town's Quaker families, some closely linked with the growth of the town. Pease and Backhouses are perhaps the most remembered, both families originally working in the textiles industry. The Backhouses were flax dressers before moving into banking, and the Pease family were in woollen fabric before adding railways, mining and engineering to their business portfolio.

11. St Cuthbert, Durham

A community of Catholics households congregated in an area of Durham's Old Elvet in the days when Catholics were viewed with suspicion. This gathering of like-minded people helped to keep their religion private, and the activities of priests could be cloaked among these houses. Gradually toleration spread and by 1791 legislation allowed Catholics to worship in public, although full emancipation was not until 1829. Old Elvet was the natural place to build a church in these liberated times and St Cuthbert's Church was completed in 1827, on a site that helped it remain tactfully discreet among the other buildings in the street. As built, there was no tower, but this was added in 1869. The architect of the original church was Ignatius Bonami, the descendant of a Venetian merchant, who after training as an architect found work in 1813 as the County Durham Surveyor of Bridges. He designed bridges at Ferryhill, Chester-le-Street and West Auckland. This experience attracted the developers of the Stockton & Darlington Railway, who employed him to design the bridge across the river at Darlington, which features in the famous painting of the opening of the railway. The Durham-based architect expanded his portfolio into grand houses and

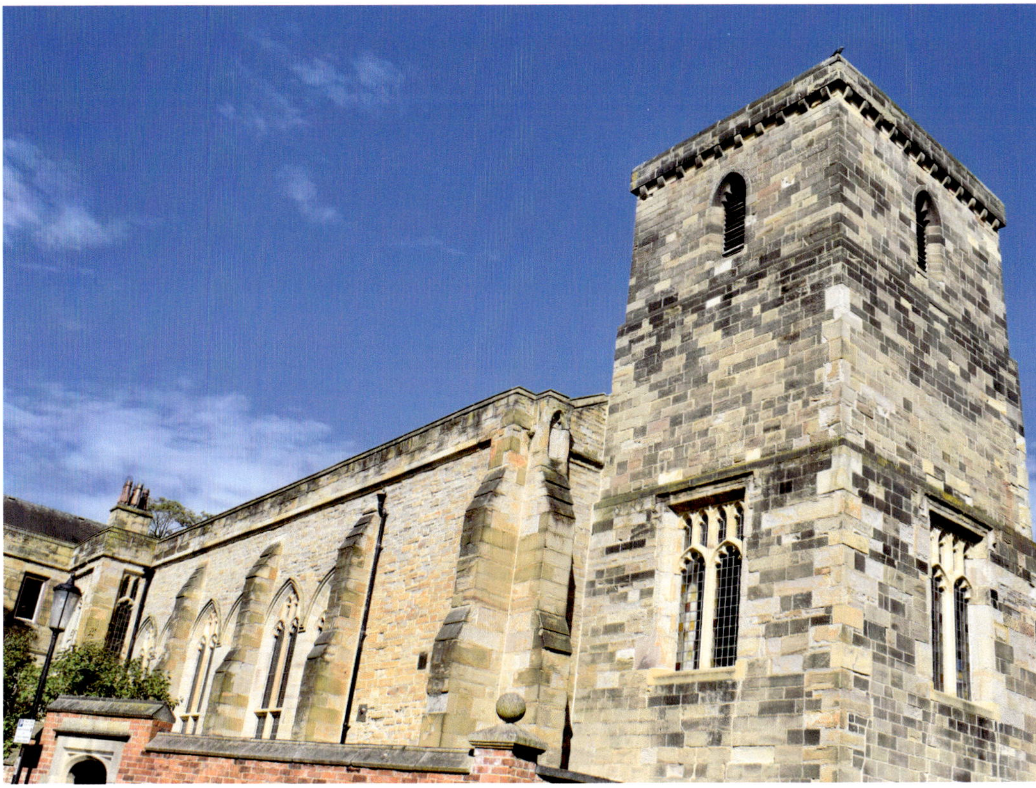

St Cuthbert, Durham.

churches. During the nineteenth century many churches were renovated and Bonami was often busy with this work including being entrusted with work at the cathedral.

12. St Oswald, Durham

Dating back to the twelfth century this church commemorates Oswald, the Northumbrian king from 633 to 642. The parish records of St Oswald's tell of the consequences of being a Catholic priest during Elizabeth I's reign. There were significant pockets of Catholics through the county and whilst they were never outlawed, the giving of mass was. Those who remained Catholic appreciated that if it was to be kept alive in the country, priests were needed. To ensure a steady flow of trained priests the English College was set up in France at Douai in 1558. When their studies were completed, the newly qualified priests started their perilous journey and, after being smuggled into the country, they travelled around preaching. They constantly faced the danger of being caught and executed. In 1590, three priests who had been ordained at Douai together with another, who had been at a college undertaking the same work in Rheims, arrived in the north. They were Edmund Duke, Richard Hill, John Hogg and Richard Holiday and they were soon under surveillance, arrested and tried in Durham. They were convicted

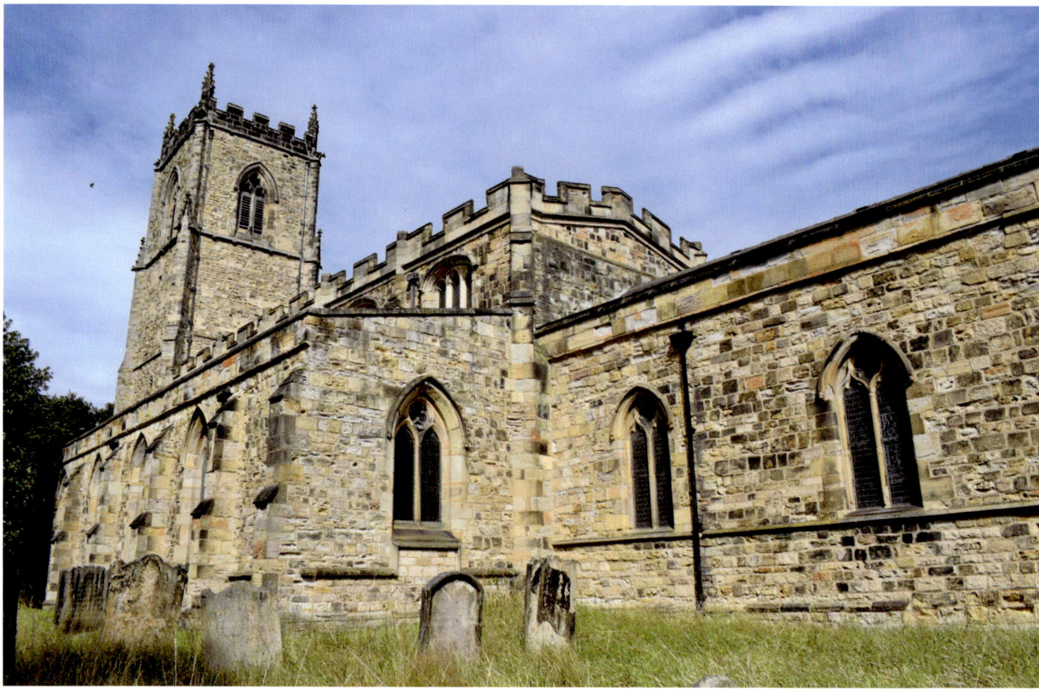

St Oswald, Durham.

and sentenced to death. St Oswald's parish register records the execution of these men and their burial. They were described as 'Popists, Traitors and Rebells' and 'hanged and quartered at Dryburn for their horrible offences'.

13. Durham Cathedral

Within the magnificent cathedral are many treasures, amongst them the shrine of St Cuthbert, whose remains were finally taken to Durham by the monks after they left Chester-le-Street fearing attack by Viking raiders. Eventually they chose the high land above a curve in the River Wear and Durham was born. How they came to Durham is the subject of legend. One story tells that Cuthbert appeared to the monks and told them to go to Durham. They had no idea where that was but met milkmaids who pointed them in the direction of Dunholme. When they arrived Cuthbert's shrine became so heavy it could not be moved and his final resting place was found. Another story suggests that Bishop Aldun had land here that he wanted to develop. A church, as a shrine, was built in the late tenth century. Things changed when the Normans arrived.

William the Conqueror had difficulty establishing his authority in the north and faced constant rebellion. In 1069 he sent troops, led by Robert Cumin, north to clear any resistance, only for them to be assassinated at Durham. The Northumbrians were joined by a Danish invasion army on board over 200 ships, and together they attacked York. William had to act; he marched north with an army, but by the time he reached York the rebels had gone, the Danes back to their ships and the Northumbrians dispersed into villages and woodland. The Danes were bribed to sail away, and William then acted to ensure there could be no further attempt to rise up against him. His troops were sent into the countryside above York to remove the unruly population and destroy their villages and livestock. This harsh retribution was the Harrying of the North. Thousands were killed and those who survived faced starvation.

William appointed Walcher as Bishop of Durham in 1071, and later Walcher was able to buy the earldom and become the Price Bishop of Durham. This secured the Norman hold over the region, as well as providing a buffer against the Scots. The Durham bishops had extensive power and authority allowing them to raise an army, issue coinage and administer justice. Bishop William de St Calais followed in 1081 and started the construction of Durham Cathedral, which was to provide a monastery for Benedictine monks. St Benedict had set out the rules that shaped monastery life at his monastery at Monte Casino in Italy in the sixth century. The monks were not allowed to own anything, but they were provided with food and clothing, and had a responsibility to look after the young, the sick and the old. Much of their time was to be devoted to prayer and meditation.

The Reformation put an end to the role of the cathedral as a monastery and much of the wealth and treasures were taken by the crown. This included stripping the gold and decoration from Cuthbert's shrine, which had been part of the cathedral. Henry VIII also started the reduction in the bishop's powers and took away the criminal jurisdiction and appointment of judges. However, the cathedral

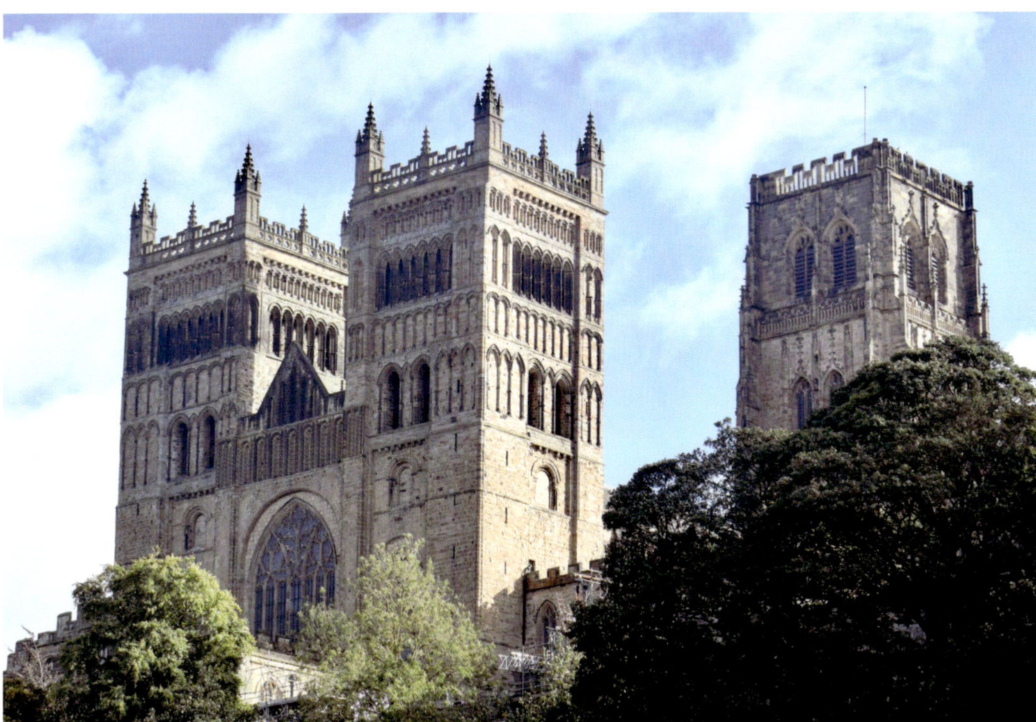

Durham Cathedral towering above the city.

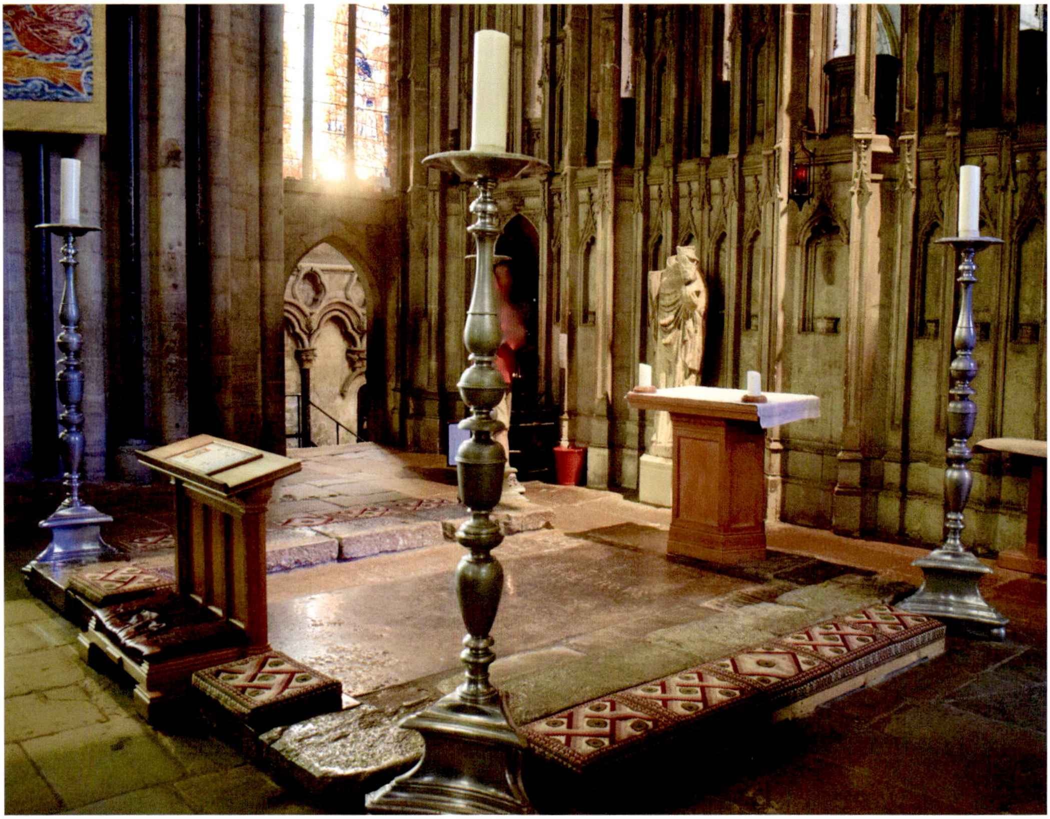

St Cuthbert's Shrine in Durham Cathedral.

was the seat of the bishop, and it was re-founded as part of the English Church without the monastic connection.

The next century brought more disruption. During the Civil War the cathedral was abused, the bishops were redundant and, to raise money for the Parliamentary cause, stonework was sold to builders. In 1646 the cathedral was used as a prison and held Scottish soldiers who had been captured at the Battle of Dundee, where Oliver Cromwell led Parliamentary forces against the Scots who were building support for Charles II. When the monarch was restored John Cosin became Durham's bishop and he set about restoring the cathedral. Now, the majestic Norman cathedral, together with the adjacent castle, form the World Heritage site above the River Wear at Durham.

14. St Edmund, Edmundbyers

In the early nineteenth century this village in the north-west of the county was described as a 'few thatched cottages scattered around a small green'. Since then, the village has developed a little but has managed to retain its character with a population still only in the hundreds. At the edge of the village stands the ancient Norman church.

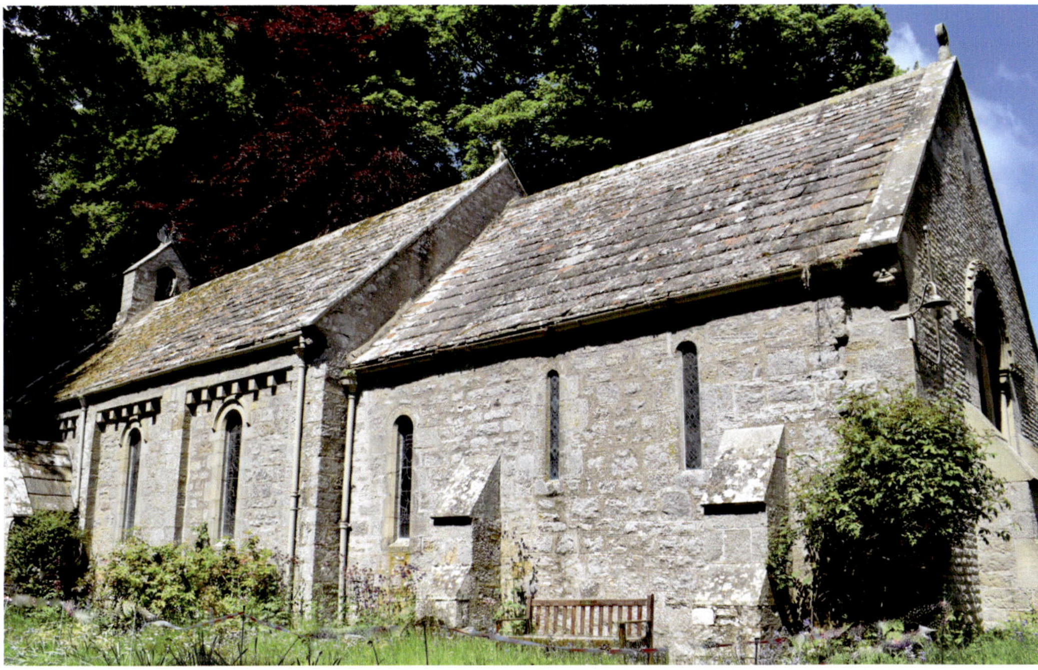

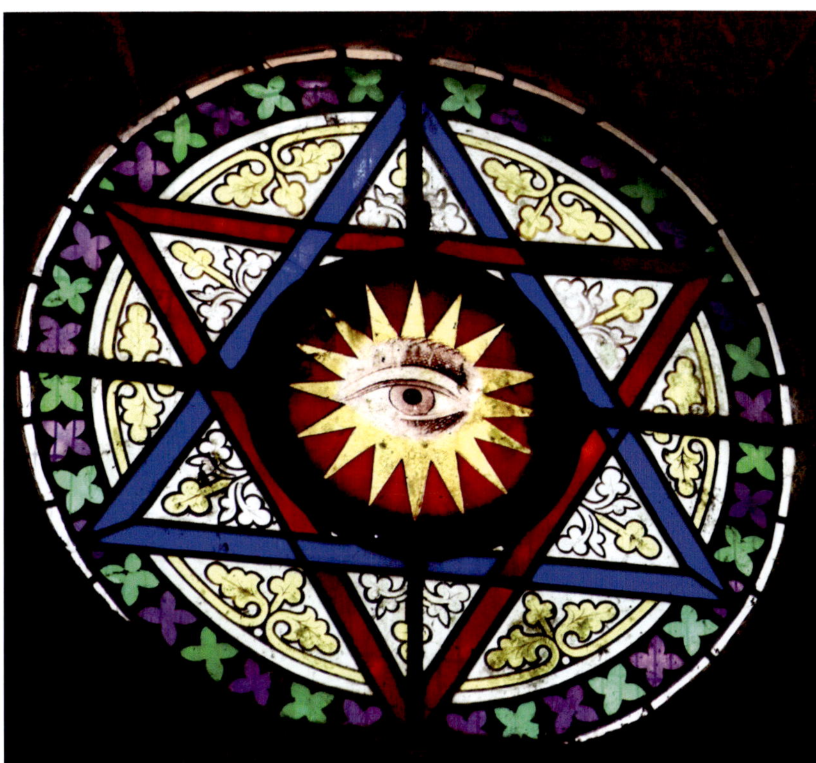

Above: St Edmund, Edmundbyers.

Right: The story goes that this window in St Edmund's Church was installed to protect against witches.

The village seems to have been troubled by witches during the seventeenth century, and a number were brought to Newcastle in 1673 to have their wrongdoing put before a judge. Evil was at work; one of the accused, Mary Hunter, was said to have transformed herself into a swallow and was seen flying around a horse cursing it. Within a week the horse was dead. Perhaps, as veterinary science was not as advanced as today, one way of rationalising illness in animals was to look for a force of evil at work in the village. With no scientific explanation, superstition and folklore could step in and witchcraft could explain much. In the close-knit communities those women who invited derision and left old scores to be settled were ideal candidates to be named as witches. The fear of witches continued into the next century. When another villager known for her malevolent acts, Elizabeth Lee, died in 1772, the story is told that the vicar, in order to protect the church, had the Eye of God window installed.

15. St John the Evangelist, Escomb

This church near Bishop Auckland dates from the late seventh century and fortunately has benefited from minimal alteration to leave it as one of the most complete Saxon churches in the country. Entry is through a porch, which was

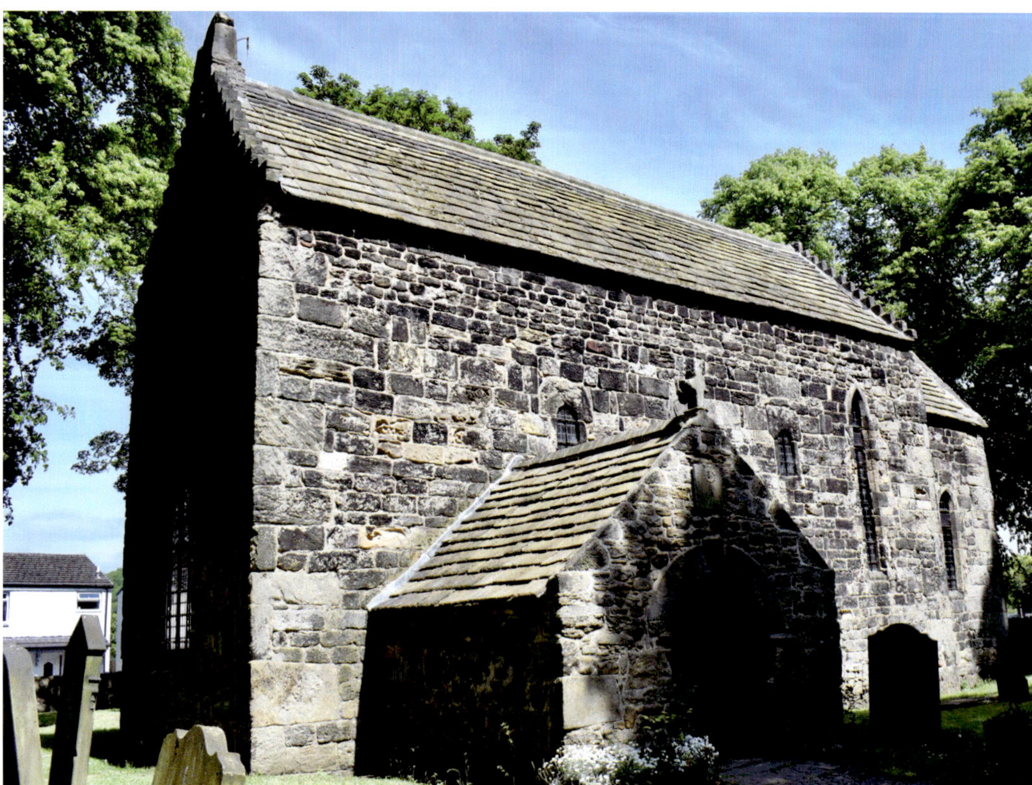

St John the Evangelist, Escomb.

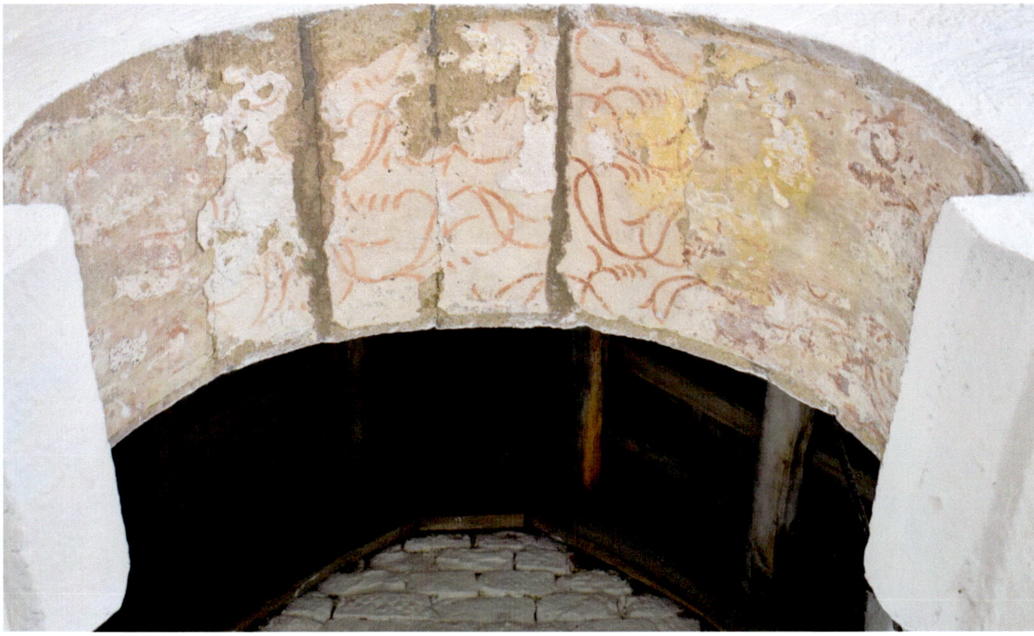

Above: Remains of decoration on the chancel arch of St John, Escomb.

Right: Narrow splayed windows in the Saxon church at Escomb.

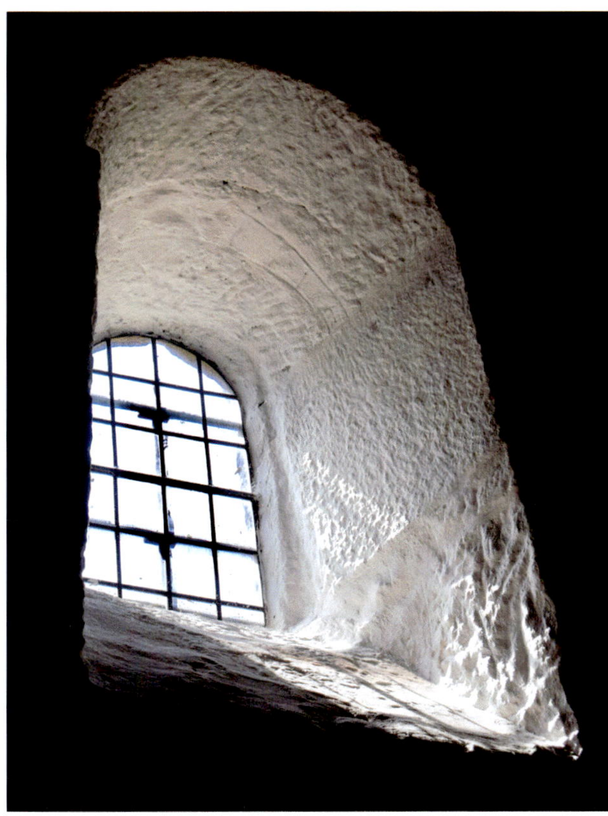

a later addition, but once inside it is back to pre-Conquest times in the narrow nave and chancel. The church incorporates stonework taken from the abandoned first-century Roman ford nearby at Binchester, so at Escomb there is still masonry in use that was crafted by Roman masons two millennia ago. This includes the chancel arch taken from the Roman fort and rebuilt inside the church. The arch displays remains of the early painting that decorated the church, although only the red colouring has survived. The church has some narrow, splayed windows that are typical of Saxon buildings; they protect against wind and rain whilst allowing some light in. Outside there is a stone that was marked 'LEG VI', again another link to the Romans and possibly the sixth legion with headquarters at York, although the elements have made this inscription difficult to see. There is also an early sundial on the south wall of the church, perhaps the earliest known in England.

The opening of ironworks and coal mines in the area brought a rapidly increasing population during the nineteenth century. The small church at Escomb

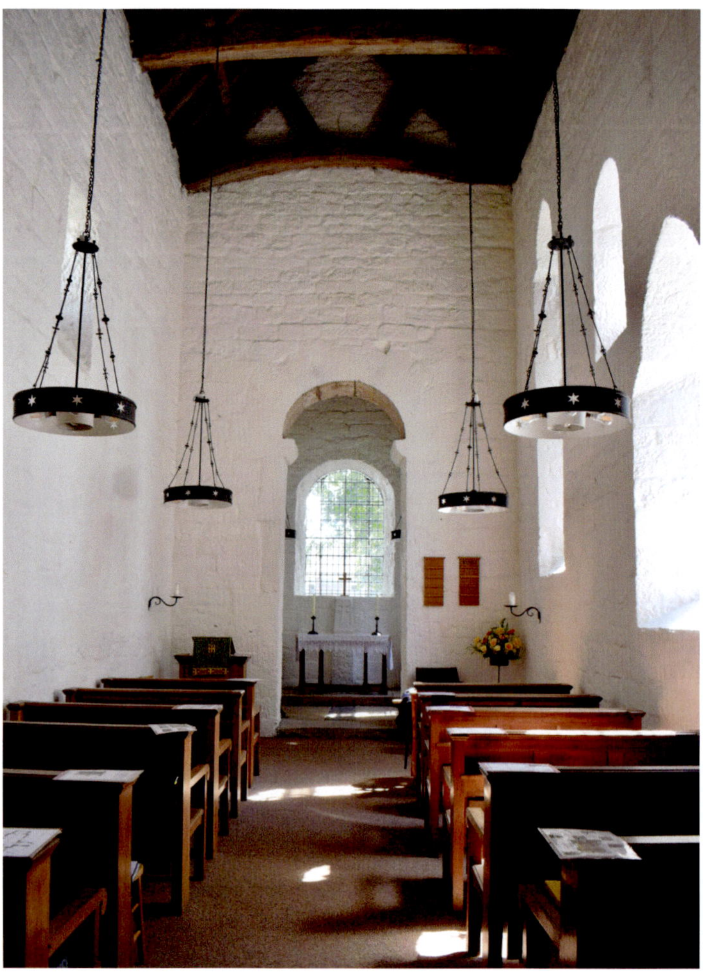

Nave and chancel arch inside St John, Escomb.

was falling into disrepair and was not adequate for the growing congregation. In 1862 builders were asked to provide estimates to build a church that would hold 300. Fortunately this church, which was consecrated in 1863, was on a new site, and no attempt has been made to enlarge or develop the early church and its surrounding graveyard. The importance of the Saxon church was not forgotten and the incumbent of the new church took steps to have it restored and preserved. It still stands whilst the Victorian church did not survive, having been demolished in the 1970s.

16. St Mary, Gainford

Symeon, a historian and monk who was active sometime around 1100, wrote a history of the See of Durham that tells of a monastery at Gainford by the early ninth century. Amongst this community was a group of stone carvers, some of whose work has been recovered and is on display inside St Mary's Church. The best-preserved example of their skill is the intricately carved Gainford Cross, which is now kept as part of the Durham Cathedral collection. There is little evidence remaining of the monastery; the church, which had been dedicated to St Cuthbert, and its lands were given to St Mary's convent in York by the local lord appointed by the Norman ruler, Guy de Balliol. The church was enlarged and the dedication changed. This is the thirteenth century church that still stands at Gainford. Like so many others it was renovated during the nineteenth century and, as part of the work, medieval grave covers were built into the north porch. Amongst the

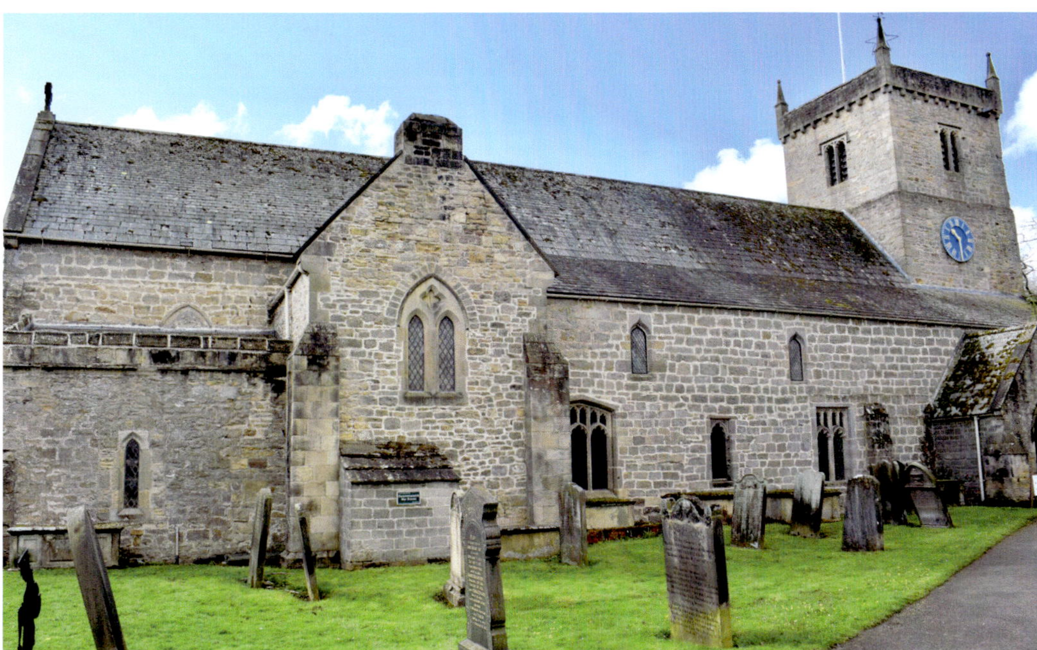

St Mary, Gainford.

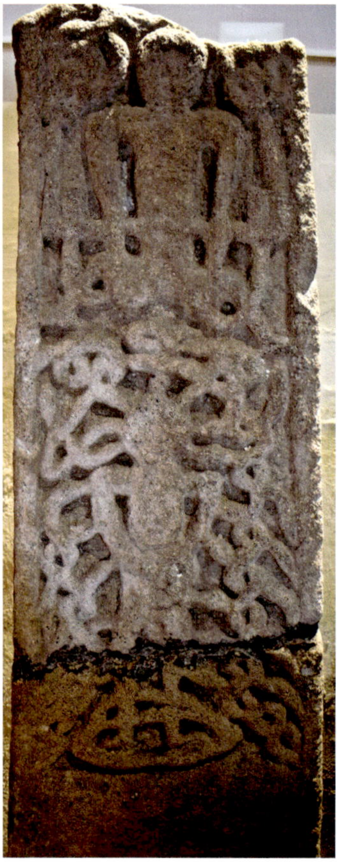

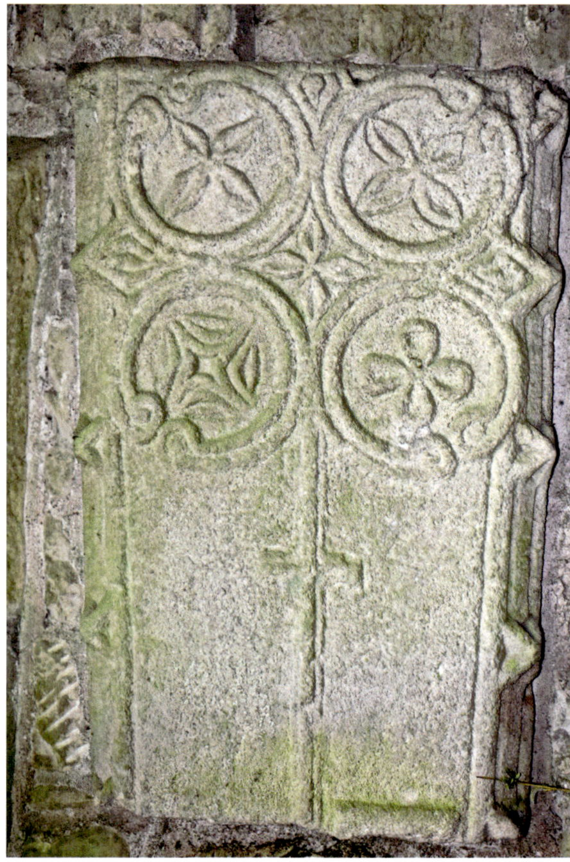

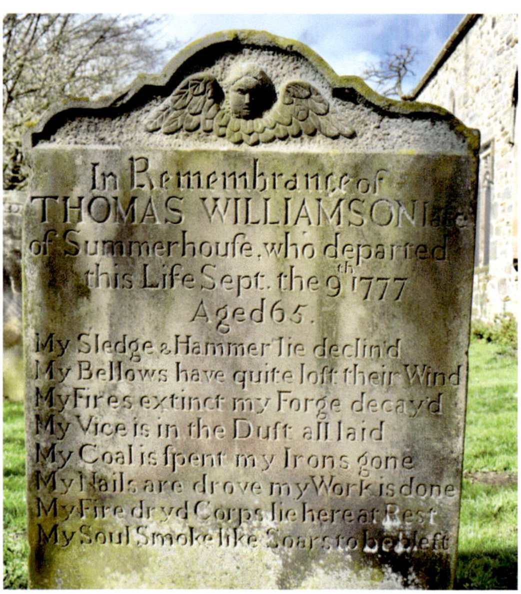

Above left: At Gainford one of the carved stones on display in St Mary's Church. This has two men enmeshed in fibrous webs.

Above right: Built into the north entrance porch at Gainford's church are many medieval grave covers.

Left: A blacksmith's grave at Gainford.

gravestones still in the churchyard one is inscribed with a poem remembering a blacksmith who was buried in 1777:

My Sledge and hammer be declin'd
My bellows have quite lost their wind
My fires extinct my forge decay'd
My vice in the dust all laid...

17. St Mary, Gateshead

The twelfth-century parish church of St Mary has been at the centre of murder, war, explosions and fires. A church on the site was the scene of the murder of Bishop Walcher in 1080. The Norman dominance was not readily accepted in the north and, whilst much of the resistance had been stamped out, a local revolt in the county saw an Anglo-Saxon leader killed. Bishop Walcher travelled to Gateshead to try to calm things but was met at the church by men intent on revenge, he was murdered and the church, which was probably wooden, was burned down. Later there was more conflict around the rebuilt church. In 1644, during the Civil War, Gateshead was occupied by troops supporting the Parliamentarian cause. They set up cannon to bombard Royalist forces holding Newcastle, and return fire destroyed the rectory and left St Mary's severely damaged.

The church suffered more damage in the nineteenth century. By this time Gateshead was transformed; industry had been attracted including ironworks and engineering

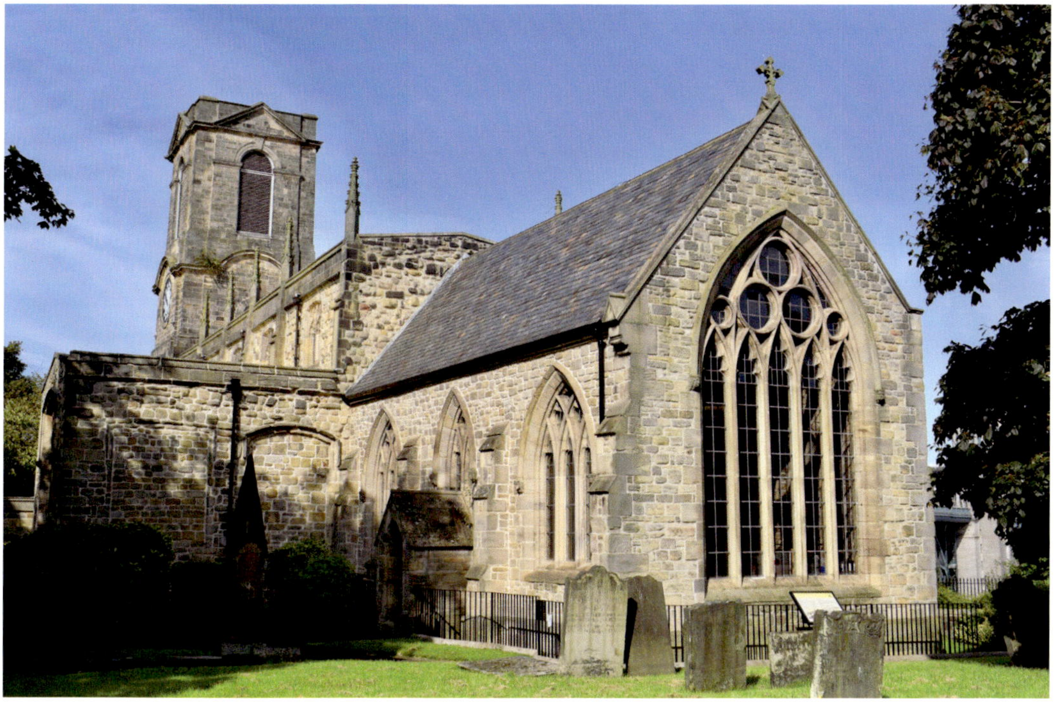

St Mary, Gateshead.

businesses, some of which were brought in by the advent of the railways. John Couthhard started building locomotives in 1839 and was followed by the Greensfield Locomotive works. Chemical works, glass manufacturers, ship building and associated trades such as rope makers were all in the town. In 1854 the church stood amongst the buildings in danger of being destroyed when a fire, which started in the textile factory of Wilson and Son, could not be controlled. It spread to a nearby chemical works, which exploded, sending molten metal and burning wood through the town. Ships moored in the river burned, hundreds were injured, and bodies were recovered from collapsed buildings. The church was wrecked. Rebuilding was entrusted to John Dobson, the Newcastle architect who produced many of the fine buildings in the city including the Central station. The church was closed in 1979 but was still not safe with two fires damaging much of the redundant building. It was repaired and served as an auction house for a time before becoming a heritage centre.

18. Gibside Chapel

As a child, Elizabeth Angela Marguerite Bowes-Lyon visited the family's Gibside estate with her father, the 14th Earl of Strathmore. However, by 1920 the family was busy transferring much of the furniture and valuables from Gibside to their home at Glamis Castle. In 1965 Elizabeth, who was by then Queen Elizabeth, the Queen Mother, was back at Gibside to hand over the chapel to the National Trust. The estate had come into the hands of the Bowes family through marriage in 1693. George Bowes, in turn, inherited it from his father in 1722. The chapel was part of George's development of Gibside. He also did much to improve the grounds with landscaping and the addition of a wing onto the grand hall, which dated from 1620. Additionally, he had a banqueting hall, orangery, and the Column of Liberty,

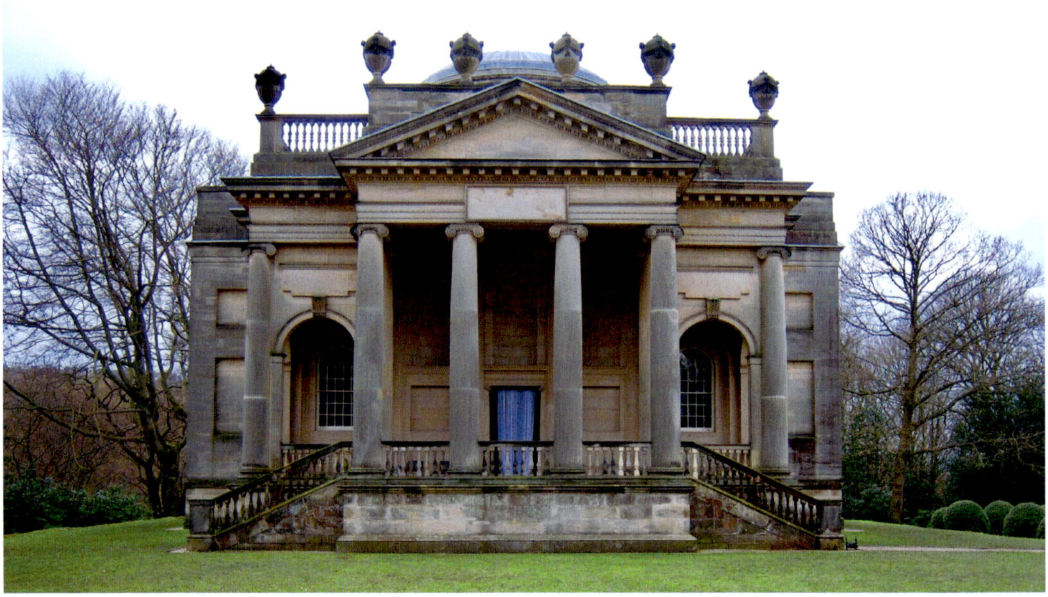

Gibside Chapel.

standing 140 feet high, built. He planned the construction of the chapel, although this was not completed until after his death. He could easily afford this extensive improvement work at Gibside with a fortune amassed from coal mining and the lucrative trade of sending ships loaded with coal down the east coast to London.

George's daughter, Mary Eleanor, inherited his fortune along with Gibside. She married the 9th Earl of Strathmore, a member of the Lyons family and the Bowes-Lyon family name emerged. After the death of her husband, Mary married again, but her second husband was a scoundrel. This was Andrew Stoney, who at one time used the hall at Gibside to hide from his creditors (he was stoney broke). The estate passed down the Bowes-Lyon family but by the early twentieth century the hall was little used, and parts of the estate were sold. The National Trust now looks after much of the estate and the restored chapel, which is approached along a splendid avenue.

19. Baptist Church, Hamsterley

The Baptists were a Protestant group that emerged in England during the years of the Civil Wars and the Commonwealth and were one of the sects that challenged the idea that the Church of England was for all the people. It seems they arrived in County Durham around 1650 when a Baptist was part of a mission to improve

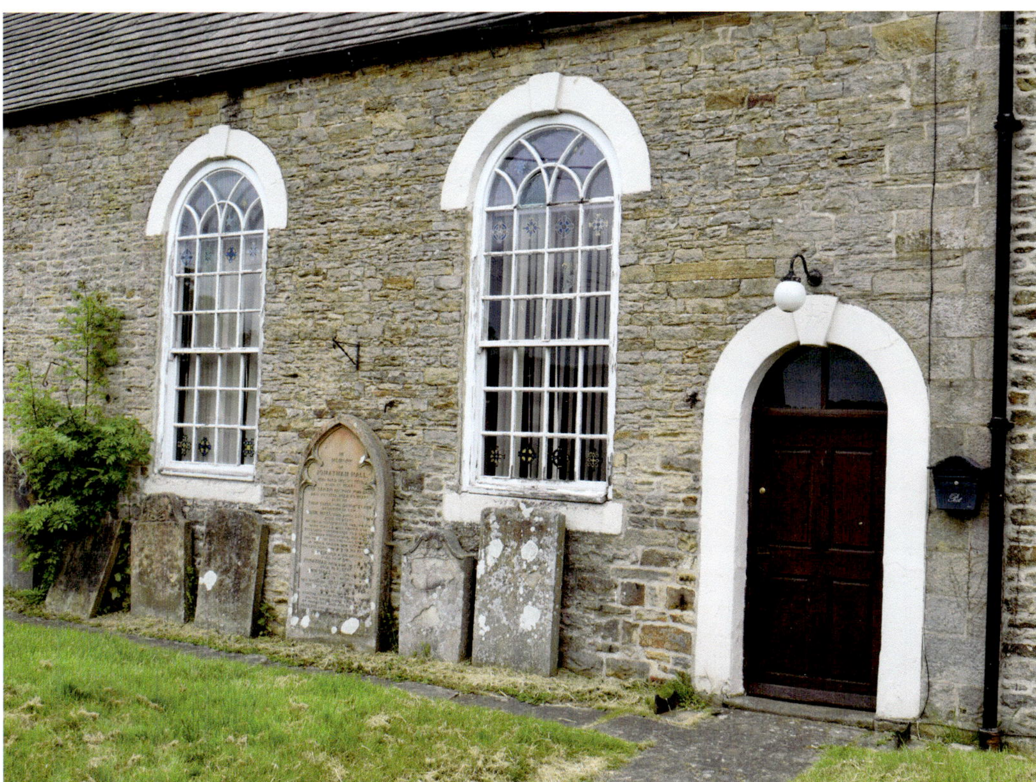

Baptist Church, Hamsterley.

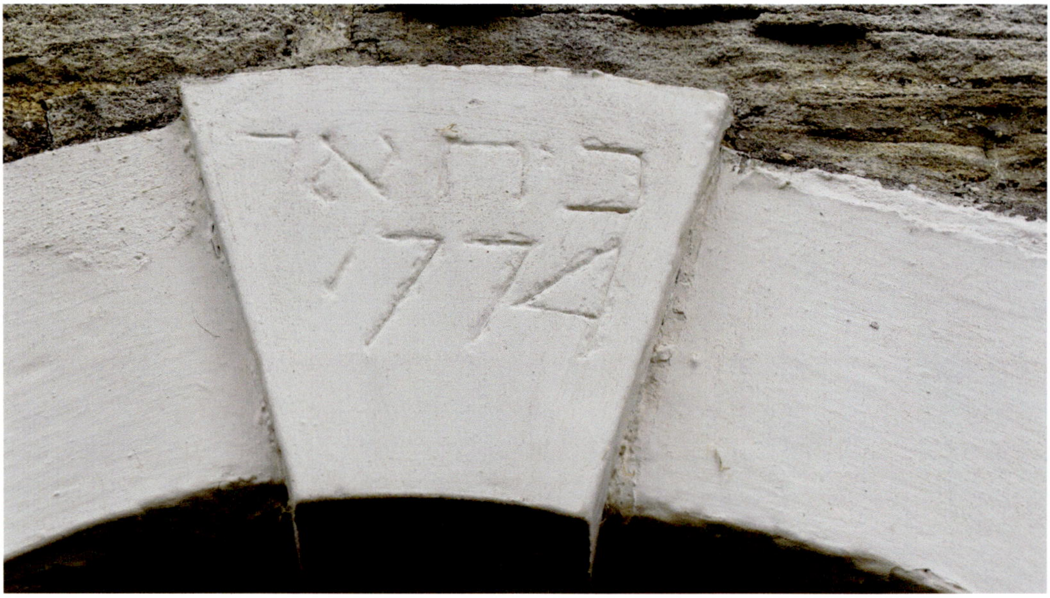

The keystone at the Hamsterley Baptist Church. Above the date is the Hebrew for Bethel or House of God.

spiritual life in the county. The villagers of Muggleswick highlighted the problem in 1642 with a petition that declared 'that we the people ... have been destitute of a preaching minister ... ever since any of us that are now breathing, were born'. They commented that a new minister had been sent but was 'the most debauched among the sons of men'. From this mission, the Baptist's influence grew. In the early days they held meetings wherever they could, including at one time in a barn near Bishop Auckland, until churches were built. Hamsterley had a Baptist chapel by 1715, although it seems this was replaced in 1774. This is the chapel that sits unobtrusively among the stone buildings in the long main street of the village, although none of the others have a collection of gravestones in the front garden.

20. St Mary Magdalene, Hart

This village near Hartlepool was once a Saxon settlement and a burial ground from that period has been found near the church; segments of crosses from this cemetery are displayed in the church. Also, inside are two fonts, one Norman and another richly carved octagonal font from the fifteenth century. There are some splendid stained-glass windows, some of which are memorials to the two world wars and a recent addition from 2018 tells the parable of the Sower from Luke chapter fifteen. The church was built in the Norman period, at the time when Robert de Brus was given the Hartness estate, which included Hartlepool and probably stretched south towards Billingham. The de Brus family established the village of Hart as the centre of the estate constructing a manor house and estate buildings. Parts of the walls of the manor buildings from this period can still be seen near the church. This was just one estate among the extensive land given

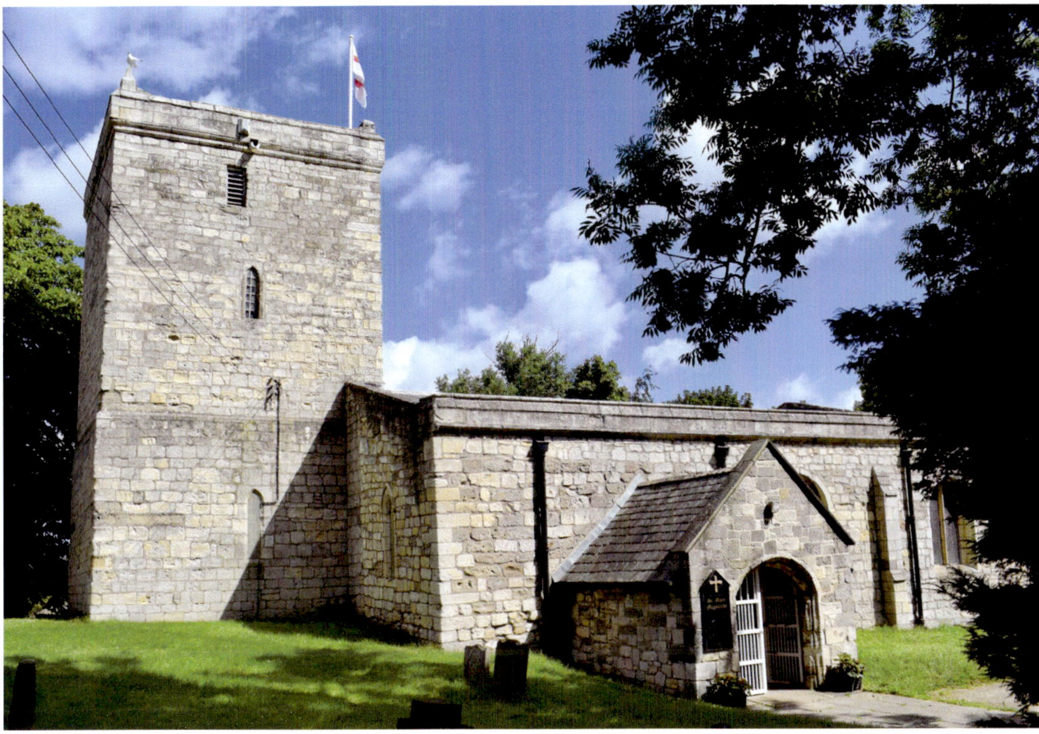

Above: St Mary Magdalene, Hart.

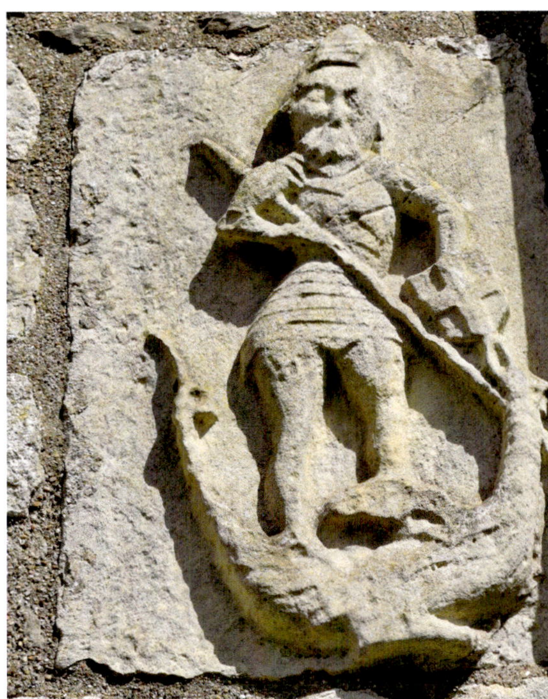

Right: Could this be George and the Dragon at St Mary Magdalene, Hart?

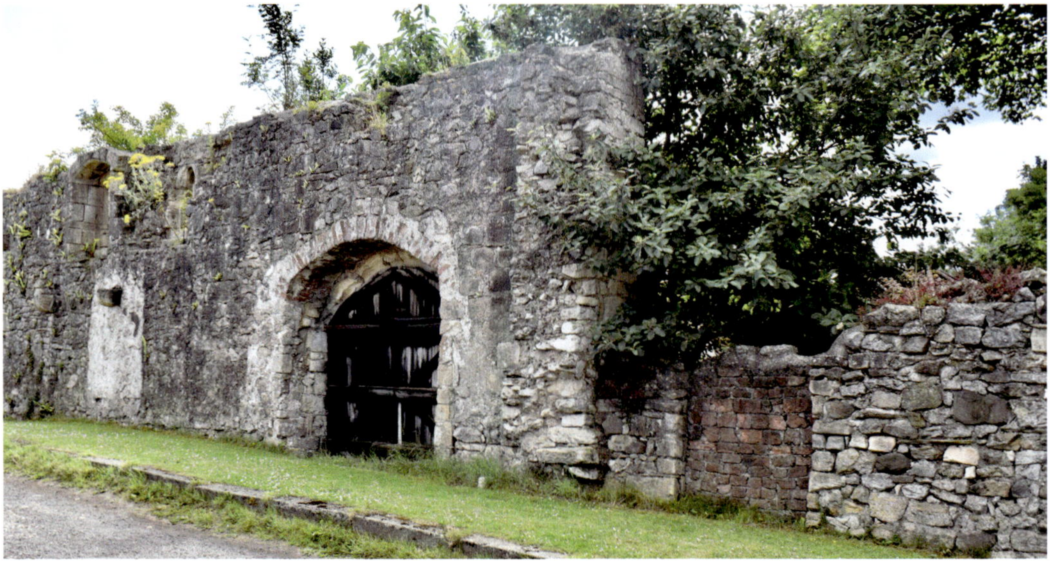

These remains of the de Brus manor buildings are close by Hart Church.

to the first Robert de Brus (Robert was a name often used by the family) who arrived from France around 1100. He was a supporter of Henry I and was given lands in the north to help strengthen Henry's position. David I, the Scottish king and brother-in-law of Henry, also gave him land at Annandale in the south of Scotland. When Henry died the English Crown was taken by his nephew Stephen. However King David had no allegiance to Stephen and decided to try to extend his territory into northern England. This brought a divided loyalty in the de Brus clan. Robert supported the English, who fought against David at the Battle of the Standard near Northallerton in 1138, whilst his son, Robert II, sided with the Scots. The estates were split; Robert kept his lands in Yorkshire whilst Annandale and Hartness went to his son, whose descendant, Robert the Bruce, was to become the Scottish king.

21. St Hilda, Hartlepool

St Hilda's Church dates to the late twelfth century. However long before this church was built the headland at Hartlepool was the site of a monastery. This was established in the 640s by Aidan the monk, who had also founded the monastery at Lindisfarne. The first abbess at Hartlepool was Heiu and when she was about to retire Aidan asked Hilda to take over. Hilda was born around 614 and was the daughter of Hereric, the nephew of Northumbria's King Edwin, and she probably lived in the royal household. Bede, the monk, writing from the twin monasteries at Jarrow and Monkwearmouth, charted the story of Britain's history from the fifth to eighth centuries in the *Ecclesiastical History of the English People,* tells that like King Edwin she was converted to Christianity by Paulinus the missionary, who was sent to England by the Pope. Hilda decided to enter a monastery in France and was on her way there when she was recalled north by Aidan. After

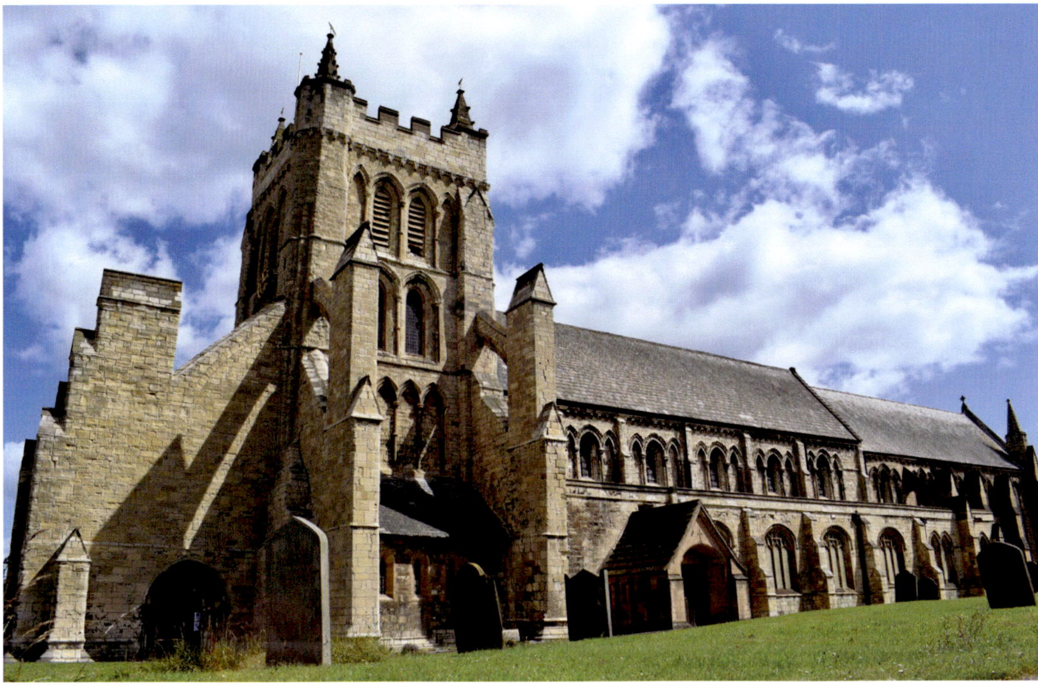

St Hilda, Hartlepool, with the heavily buttressed tower.

spending time in Hartlepool, Hilda moved to the abbey at Whitby and from there she founded another a little further south at Hackness.

Later, the de Brus family became associated with Hartlepool, which was just part of their extensive land holdings. The settlement on the headland had the advantage of becoming a busy port serving much of the county. The church at Hart was no longer adequate to serve this community and, as a display of the prosperity brought by the commercial port, work on the grand church dedicated to St Hilda was started in 1190.One external feature of the church is the buttressing, which had to be was added in 1230 to make the tower secure.

22. St Michael, Heighington

This Norman church is set in the centre of the village green. Like so many churches its historical value has been recognised and it has been given Grade I listed status along with some of the other exceptional churches in the county. The church has a grand Norman arch dividing the nave and chancel. Inside there are other reminders its heritage: the pulpit dates to the years before the Reformation and the font dates to around the fourteenth century, as do the two female effigies standing near the entrance. There is a plaque in memory of William Pryce Cumby, the grandson of a church warden at Heighington, who went to sea when he was only eight years old and went on to forge a distinguished career. He was serving as a lieutenant aboard one of the ships fighting the French at the Battle of Trafalgar. After his captain was killed, he took over, repelled boarders and went on to take the enemy ship.

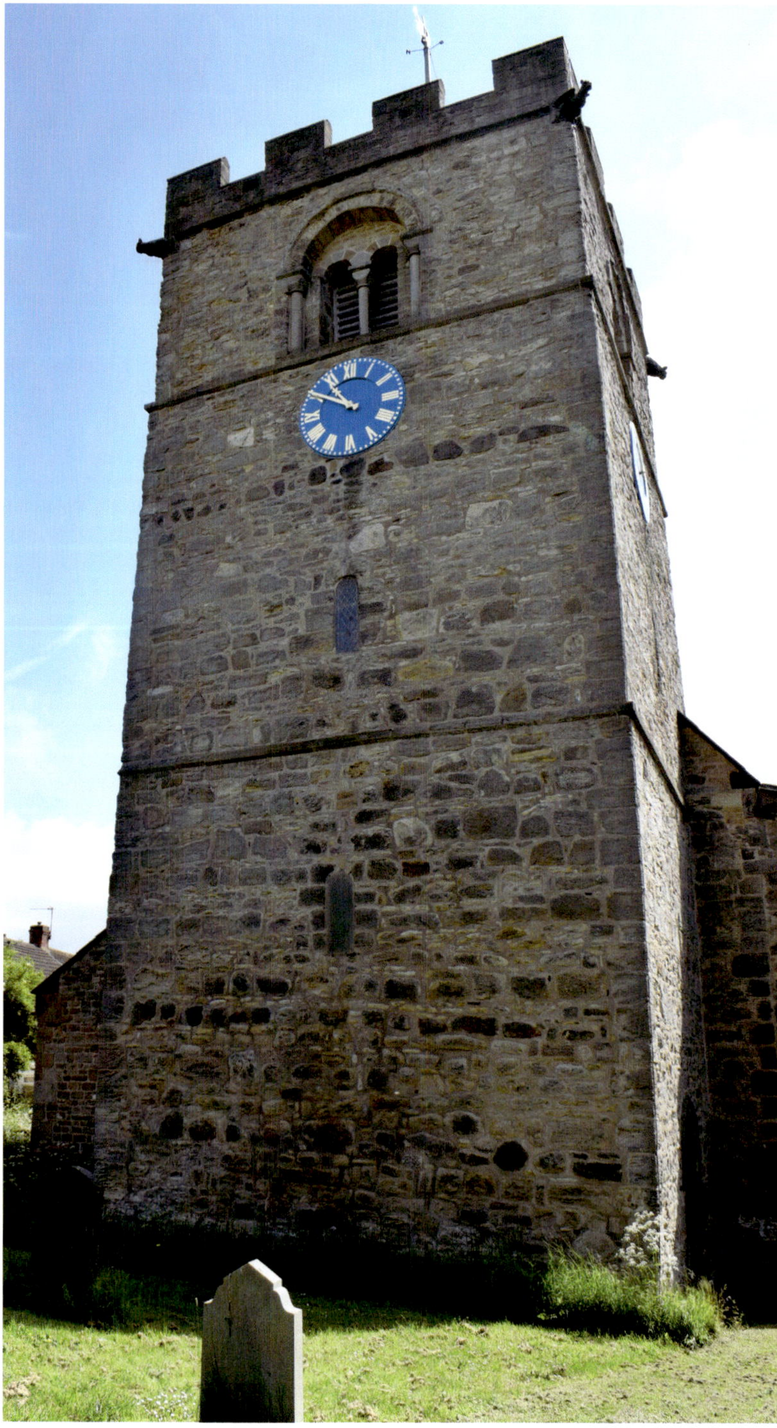

The Norman tower at St Michael, Heighington.

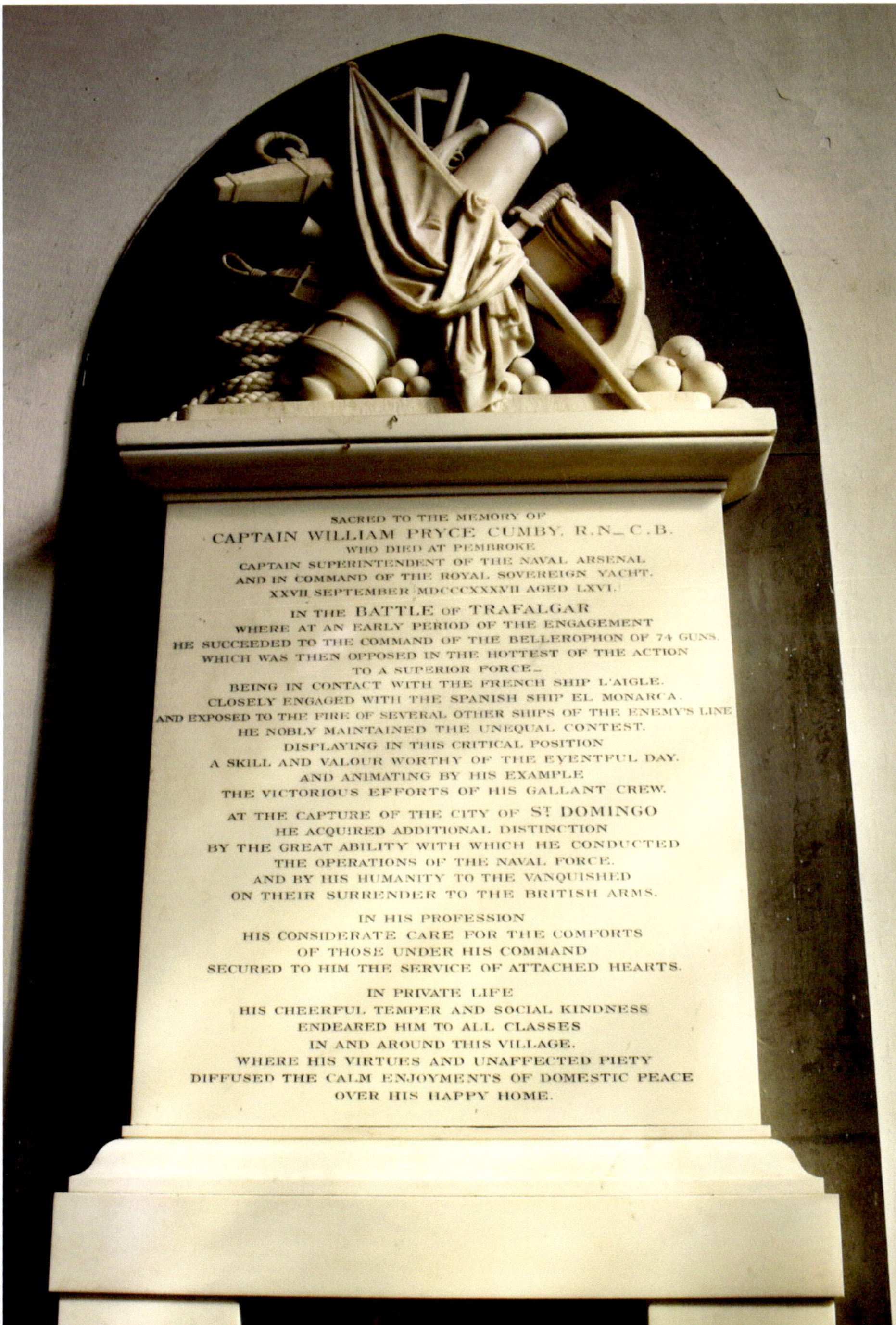

The naval decoration on this memorial in the church at Heighington remembers Captain Willam Pryce Cumby, a hero of Trafalgar.

23. Hetton-le-Hole Methodists

To the north of the county the start of deep mining in the area was made possible with the advancing technology and design of mines. Flooding could be a problem, but steam engines were employed to draw water and ventilation was aided by sinking two shafts. In 1819 the Hetton Coal Co. leased land from John Lyons (a member of the Bowes-Lyons family) and set about drilling through the thick layer of stone to reach the coal. When this was broken through, coal started to be brought out of the pit to be transported by the newly opened Hetton Railway. This was engineered by George Stephenson and covered the 8 miles to the docks at Sunderland. It was designed to use locomotives, although on some inclines the wagons were hauled up on ropes attached to stationary engines or allowed to run down the slopes before being reattached to a locomotive. An influx of miners and their families saw the little hamlet of Hetton-le-Hole start to develop and Methodists were soon providing for the growing congregation. A Wesleyan

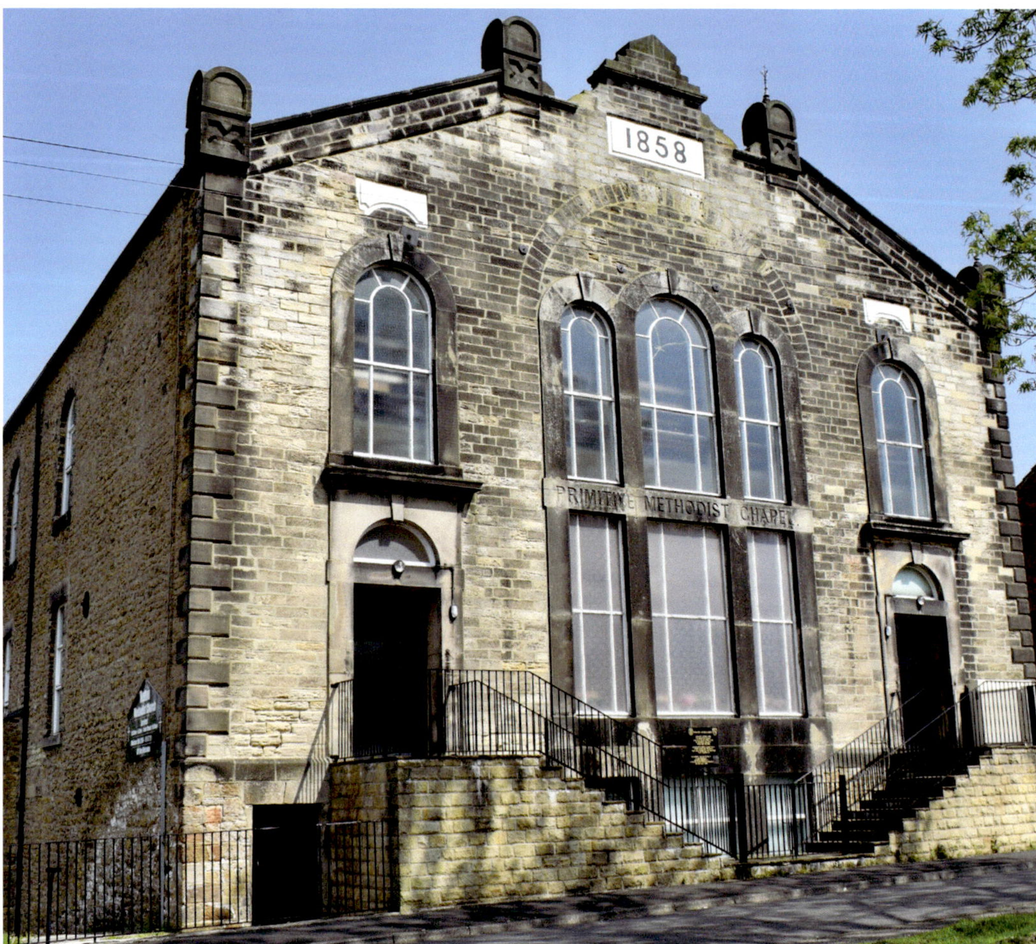

The Methodist Church at Hetton-le-Hole.

Methodists church was opened in 1824. By this time, the Methodist movement had started to split into sects and, to distinguish themselves from others, the original movement adopted the term Wesleyan. The Primitive Methodist were formed in 1811. This group was initially formed by William Cloves and Hugh Bourne, who often attracted large gatherings to their open-air meetings. However, the grandees of the Methodist organisation no longer favoured outdoor preaching and frowned on this work by these laymen and ordered them to stop. When they could not reconcile with the main body of Methodists, they broke away to find the group taking a name which looked back to the work and custom of preaching in the open air established by Wesley. These Primitive Methodists also became known as Ranters because of their loud preaching in public places; in 1823 a report told of Ranters preaching in Durham Market Place. A Primitive Methodist Chapel came to Hetton in 1858 but before then preachers from this sect would visit. In 1834 two preachers met a terrible fate as they approached the village. John Brantford and John Hewson were walking along the railway, deep in conversation, when the wagoner shouted at them to watch out. Wagons were starting to be run up and down the hill and one caught Hewson, who was knocked over and crushed to death by the wagon wheels. Trying to avoid the wagons, Brantford tripped over one of the ropes, fell onto the line and had both legs broken as the wagons ran over him. He only managed to survive into the evening.

24. St Edwin, High Coniscliffe

This long church standing above the River Tees dates from the thirteenth century, although there was probably another church on the site in the previous century. The unusual octagonal spire was added in the fourteenth century. Above the church door is a stone with a carving of a lamb and cross with the inscription 'AGNU', a reference to Agnus Dei, the lamb of God. It is referred to as the Saxon stone, although it is thought to be from an earlier period and was originally part of the nearby Roman fort at Piercebridge.

A church dedicated to St Edwin is unusual and the story of Edwin takes us back to Northumbria in the Dark Ages and Bede's retelling of history. The division of the country into kingdoms brought conflict when those looking to increase their territory came against those defending their lands. Bede relates stories about Edwin and his fight to claim his birth right. Edwin's father, Aelle, was the King of Diera (the lands from Tees to the Humber), but on his death Aethelfrith, the King of Bernica (southern Scotland to the Tees), swooped and took control, leaving Edwin in exile and seeking hospitality in other royal households. He spent time in Wales and Mercia (Midlands) where he fathered two children, Osfrith and Edfrith, by Cweberga, the daughter of the Mercian king. He was always aware of his right to the northern kingdom, as was Aethelfrith, who, in order to secure his position, plotted to have Edwin assassinated. The plan failed but Edwin had to react. In 616 Raedwald, the East Anglian king, came to Edwin's aid, mustering an army that defeated Aethelfrith to restore Edwin to his Northumbrian kingdom.

The story now turns to the conversion of Edwin and how he eventually became a Christian. He chose to marry Ethelburga, the daughter of the King of Kent. She was a Christian and Edwin undertook to take instruction with a view to converting. In the meantime, to prevent Ethelburga being corrupted she was accompanied north by Paulinus, a missionary who had been sent to England by the Pope. In 626 another attempt on Edwin's life was foiled when an aide stepped in and took the force of the attackers poisoned knife. Edwin, however, was wounded and vowed that if he survived his injury and was able to defeat the West Saxon king who had ordered the assassination attempt, he would become a Christian. He recovered, gathered his army, and defeated the West Saxon king. He had been blessed with good fortune and in 627 he was baptised at York to become the first Christian king of Northumbria. Edwin survived for six years, but was killed fighting the joint forces of Cadwallon, the king of Gwynedd (north Wales), and Penda, the King of Mercia, who resisted Edwin's continuous attacks as he sought to expand the Northumbrian kingdom. Penda had remained a pagan and Edwin was seen as a Christian martyr and sainthood followed.

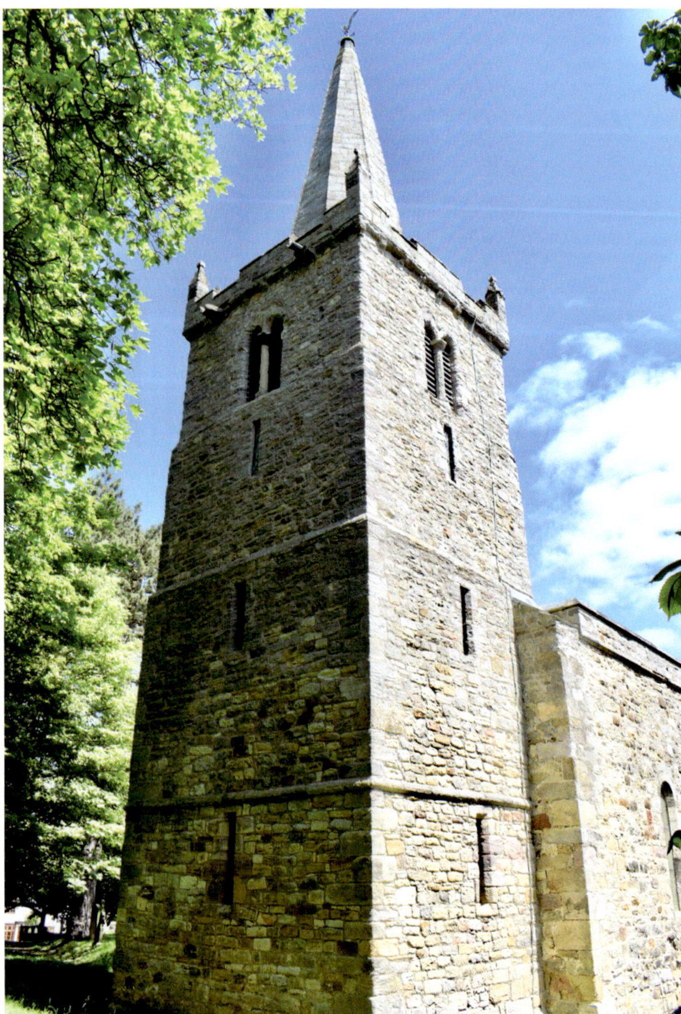

St Edwin, High Coniscliffe, a Norman church extended in the thirteenth century when the tower was added, followed in the next century with the spire.

25. Christ Church, Jarrow

From 1852 Palmers Shipyard and Ironworks was offering work and this attracted families to the town. Jarrow was served by the ancient St Peter's Church and to cater for the growing congregation the rebuilding was announced in 1864. However, the development was not enough, and another church was needed. The foundation stone of Christ Church was laid in 1868 and in October of the following year the church, which had cost around £4,000, was opened.

Almost seventy years later the news was not so good. In October 1936, a blessing was given in Christ Church for the Jarrow Marchers, who were setting off for London to present a petition to the government demanding action to relieve the distress caused by unemployment in the town. The marchers were led out of the

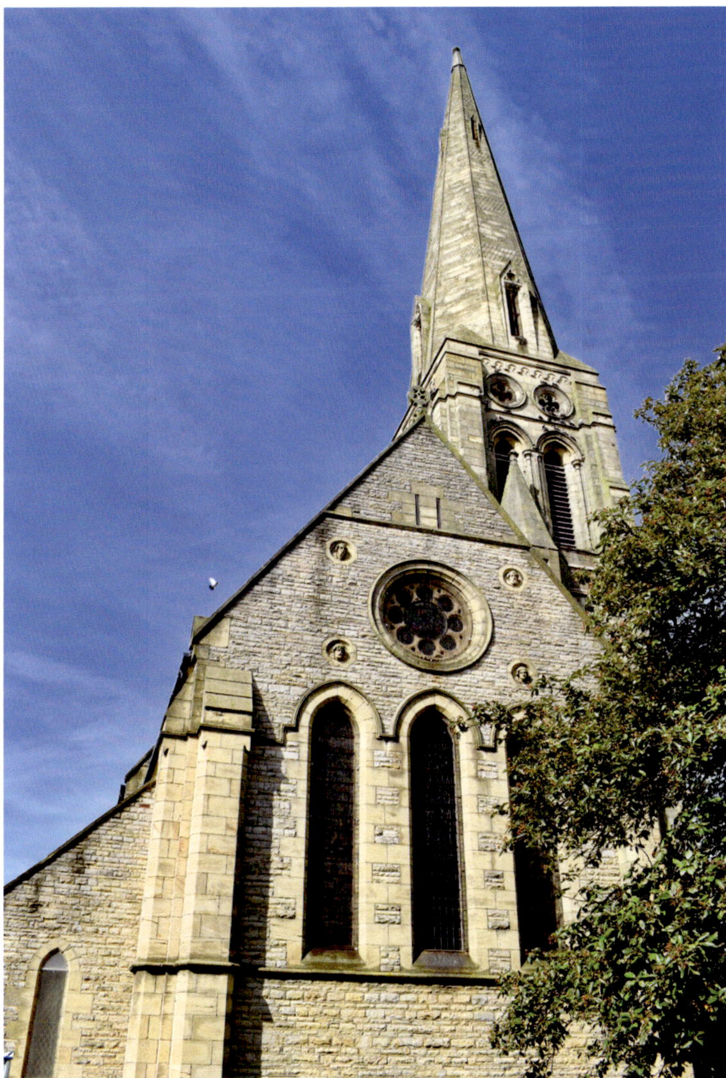

Christ Church, Jarrow.

town by their MP, Ellen Wilkinson, and the mayor. A few days later Ellen was at the Labour Party Conference demanding the government be forced to act so that 'our people shall not be starved ... and our children will not die'. The inter-war years are associated with depression and unemployment and Jarrow was badly hit. Palmers Shipyard had provided work for thousands, but shipbuilders were severely affected by the downturn. After an initial boom, as fleets were rebuilt after the First World War, the world faced economic depression and shipbuilding was one of the casualties. The last ships left from Palmers in 1932; without new orders Palmers was bankrupt. The final blow came in 1934 when the yard was bought by the National Shipbuilders Security, a government-backed body tasked to rationalise the country's shipbuilding by buying and dismantling unprofitable yards. There was little work and J. B. Priestley, who wrote about his tour of the country in the early 1930s in his book *English Journey*, told of his visit to Jarrow where he found a 'derelict town' and by the river 'tumble down sheds, rotting piles, coal dust and mud'.

So, the march was organised to highlight the plight of the people of Jarrow and progressed to Chester-le-Street, Ferryhill and Darlington before moving south to reach London by the end of October. Whist the march did highlight the plight of many in the town there was little aid provided. It was the rearmament of the country's defences against the growing threat from Hitler's regime that brought some work.

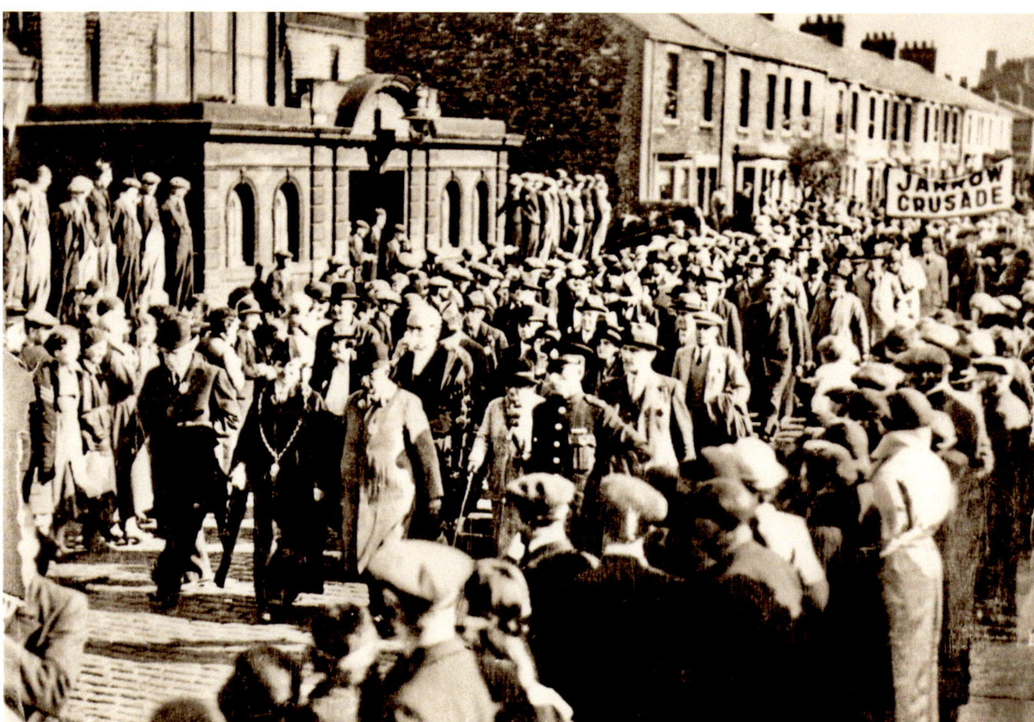

The start of the Jarrow March near Christ Church in Grange Road West.

26. St Paul, Jarrow, and 27. St Peter, Monkwearmouth, Sunderland

This is the story of two connected churches both founded by a nobleman who chose to become a monk. In 674 King Ecgfrith of Northumbria gave Benedict Biscop land on the northern banks of the River Wear to establish a monastery. A narrow Saxon church was the first building, but more followed including chapels and domestic buildings needed to support the monastery life. Today the church, which has been remodelled and extended over the centuries, is surrounded by open space. Maps from the nineteenth century show buildings encroaching on

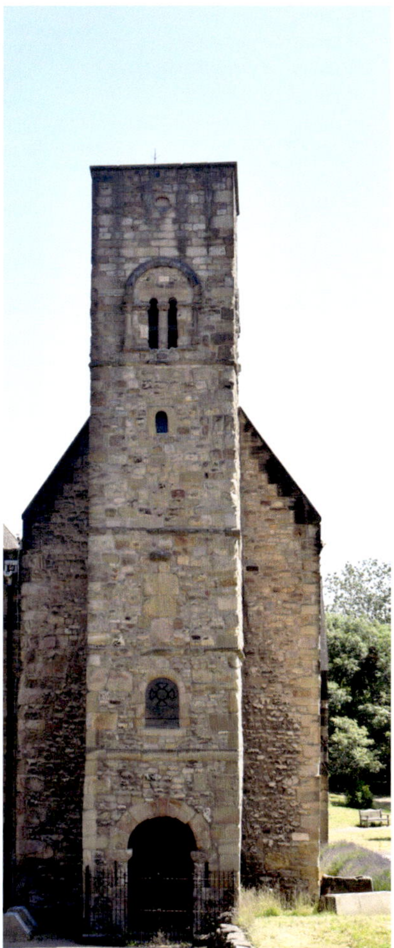

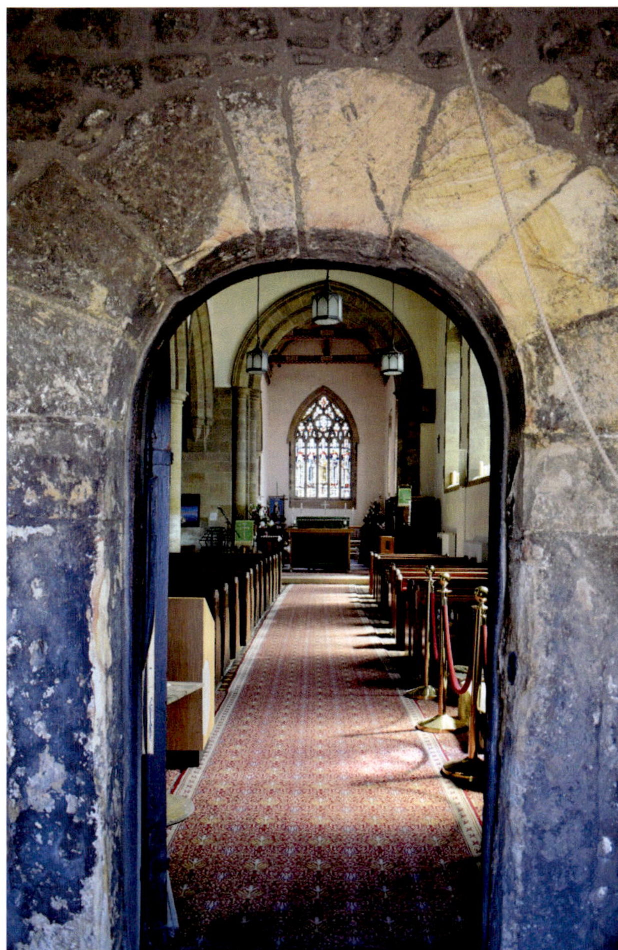

Above left: St Peter's Church, Monkwearmouth. The church incorporates this western wall and porch of the original Saxon church that was part of the monastery founded by Benedict Biscop. The upper part of the tower was an eleventh-century addition.

Above right: The Saxon entrance porch at St Peter, Monkweamouth, Sunderland.

the church but the site has now been cleared and excavations have allowed the outline of the monastery buildings to be marked on the ground.

A few years later King Ecgfrith granted more land to Biscop, this time a little further north, and a second monastery was built at Jarrow. On this site is St Paul's Church, built around the chancel of the Saxon church, which was part of the early monastery complex. These religious communities became centres of learning. The Venerable Bede is perhaps the most remembered scholar; he spent much of his life between the two monasteries writing. His works included the *Ecclesiastical History of the English People*. In this book Bede records how Christianity was brought back to the country. After the Roman legions departed England and the Anglo-Saxons arrived from northern Europe, they brought with them their worship pf pagan gods to challenge the Christian faith that had been established during Roman times. Despite the decline in Christianity there was a gradual conversion of these invaders during the seventh century and Christianity was reinvigorated. Bede tells how Pope Gregory had 'a deep desire to save our nation' and goes on to explain how Gregory became aware of the need for help when he visited a marketplace in Rome and saw slave boys for sale. He was told they came from Britain, and he enquired 'whether the islanders are Christian or whether they are ignorant heathens'. He was informed they were pagans, and the boys came from Diera, which covered lands from the Tees to the Humber. (Eventually Diera would merge with Bernica, which stretched from southern Scotland to the River

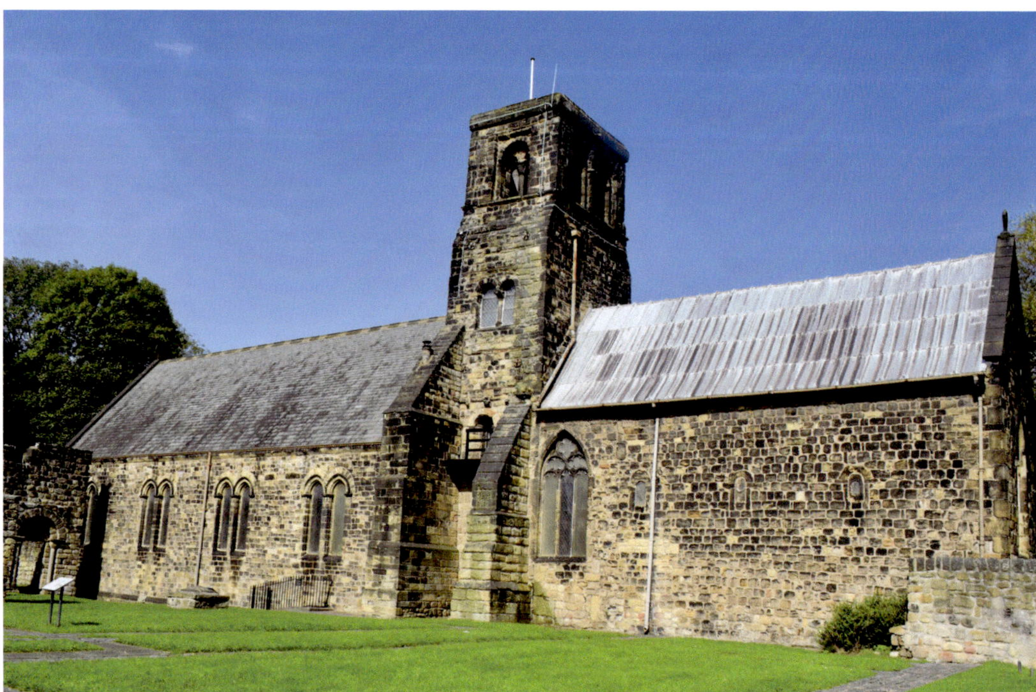

St Paul's Church at Jarrow. The eastern section (the right of the picture) is the surviving part of the monastery church.

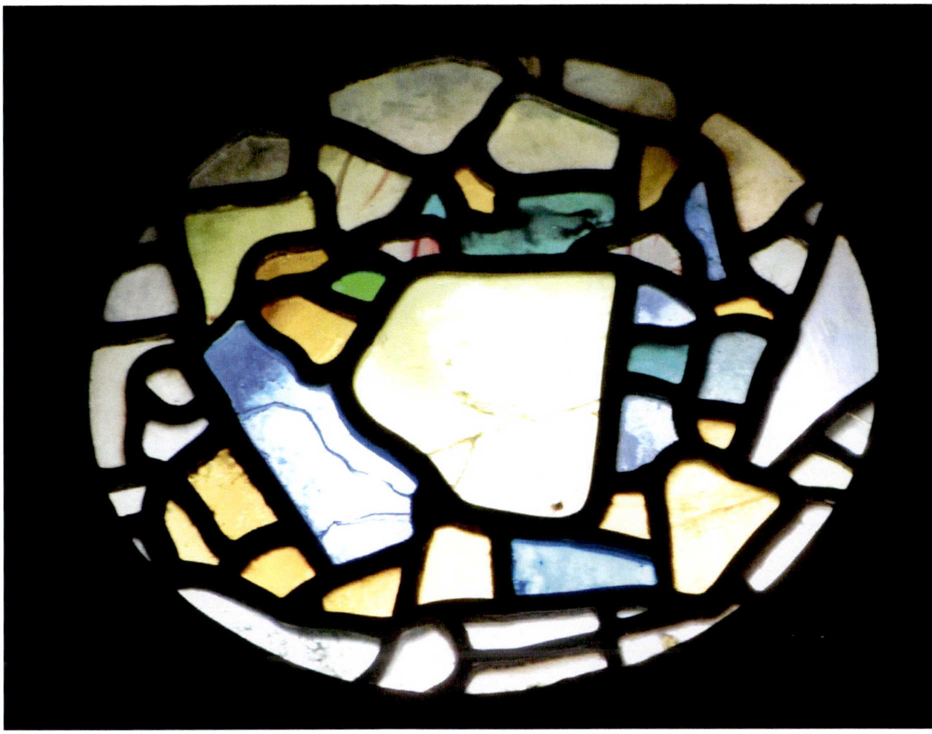

Above: The stained-glass window at Jarrow has been made from fragments of Saxon glass excavated on the site.

Right: Displayed in the ancient chancel of St Paul's, Jarrow, is Bede's Chair, although the eighth-century monk would never have sat in this medieval piece.

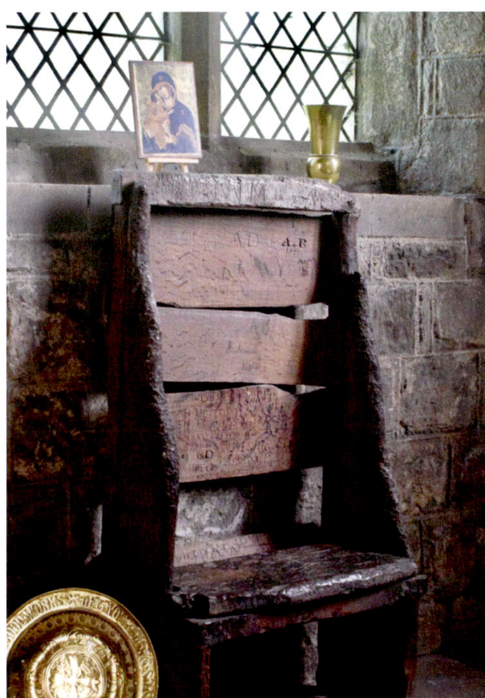

Tees, to form Northumbria). This news spurred Gregory to send missionaries to rescue the country 'from wrath ... and [be] called to the mercy of Christ'.

The history of the two monastery sites follows similar patterns. By the mid-ninth century they had been abandoned, either to escape the threat of attack or suffering the same fate as others, for example at Lindisfarne and Whitby where Viking raiders attacked and looted. The existence and importance of the monasteries was not forgotten, and they were re-established by the Normans for Benedictine monks who were connected to Durham Cathedral.

History was to repeat itself and the monasteries did not survive. This time it was the work of Henry VIII who decided to investigate the monasteries and sent out agents to find, or it can be suggested they were encouraged to find, some evidence of 'criminal' activity. The results of the investigations were summarised in the Compendium Competorum. At Jarrow it was noted there were only eight monks but two had been guilty of some scandalous activity. The Act of Suppression of 1536 required all monasteries with income under £200 per year to be closed and their lands forfeit to the Crown. As Jarrow was reported to have an income of only £40 and Monkwearmouth even less, they were closed. Preserved at Jarrow, beside St Paul's Church are the ruins of the medieval monastery.

Both churches display items from their long history. At Monkwearmouth there are carving from the era before the Norman Conquest, while at Jarrow there is a small stained-glass windrow made from glass fragments of glass dated to the Saxon period.

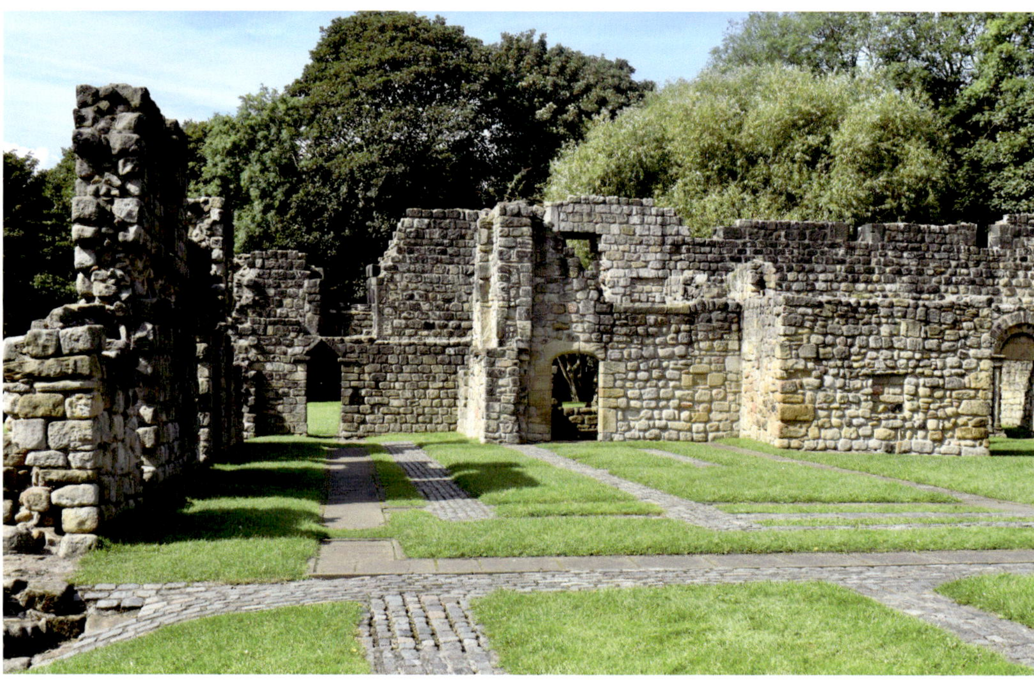

After the Norman invasion the monastery at Jarrow was re-founded. These are the remains beside St Paul's Church.

28. St Helen, Kelloe

In the hamlet of Kelloe, set in a valley, this church dates back to Norman times with work starting in the late eleventh/early twelfth centuries. On display inside the church is a carved cross that had once been incorporated into the church walls. It is now restored and stands in the chancel. The carving tells the story of St Helen and how she was guided to find the true cross on which Jesus was crucified. She was the mother of Constantine the Great, the Roman Emperor between 306 and 387. Helen undertook a pilgrimage to the religious sites of the Holy Land and in Jerusalem found the true cross.

Elizabeth Barrett Browning spent her early years at the grand Coxhoe Hall where her parents had moved to from the Caribbean and the sugar plantation owned by her father. She was christened at the church in 1808 but her connection with Kelloe was short lived as the family moved to an estate in Herefordshire a year later.

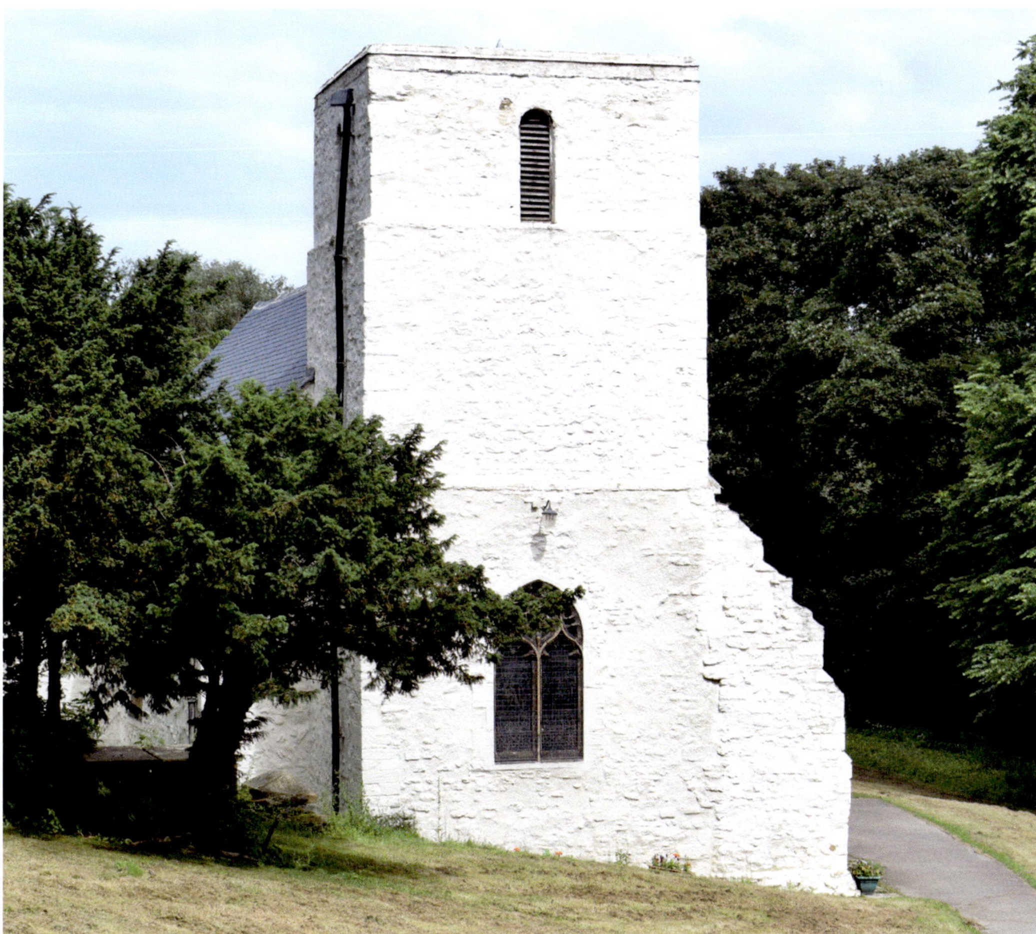

St Helen, Kelloe.

29. St John the Evangelist, Kirk Merrington

By the nineteenth century, the Norman church at Kirk Merrington, near Spennymoor, was in poor condition and even the tower was in danger of collapsing. A radical rebuilding program was started. The work was completed by 1852 and, whilst the external structure was rebuilt, inside the church much of the furniture dating back to the 1600s has been retained.

The strategic position of the church, on a hilltop commanding sweeping views over the countryside, was recognised in 1144 by William Cumin when he retreated from Durham and fortified the church. This was the final episode in his attempt to usurp the Bishopric of Durham. Cumin was a high-ranking official in Scotland's royal court where King David I had ambitions to extend his kingdom into northern England. David's attempt to increase his holdings into England had been halted at the Battle of the Standard near Northallerton. He did retain Cumberland and Northumberland but still harboured ambitions south of the Tyne. On the death of Durham's Bishop Rufus in 1141 he saw an opportunity to extend his influence by supporting his Chancellor, William Cumin, in an attempt to take over the role of bishop. At Durham, Cumin was able to gather support from many of the local barons, who felt some allegiance to the Scottish king or, seeing his growing reach into the north, wanted to safeguard their position and land holdings. The barons, in those feudal times, held their land under the bishop and in return provided military

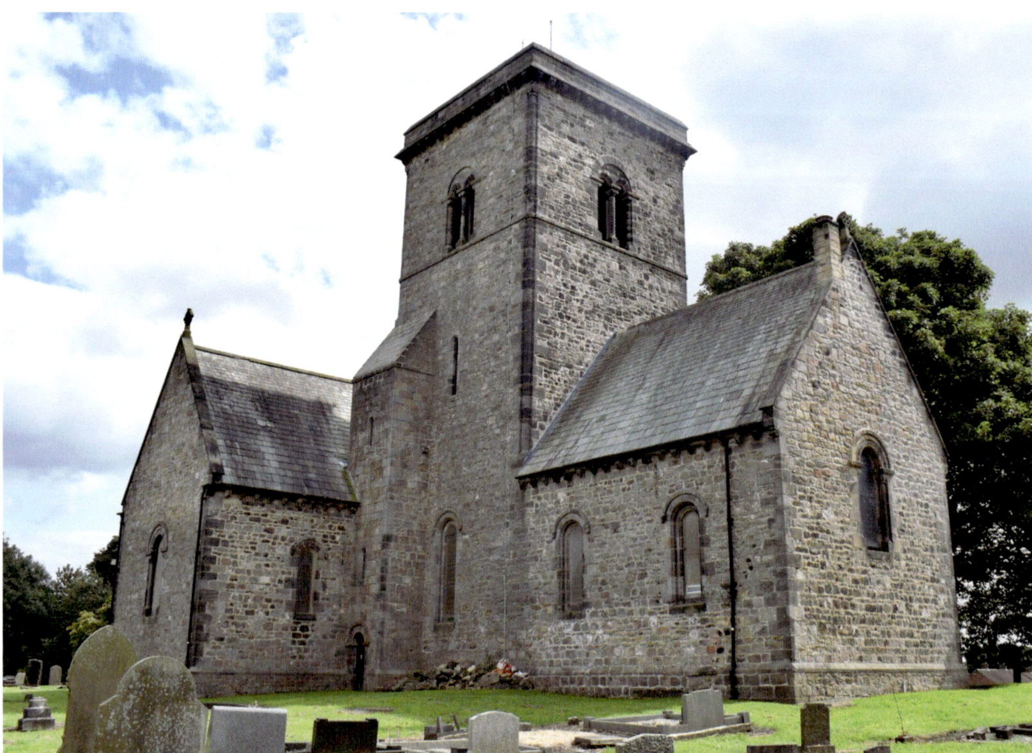

St John the Evangelist, Kirk Merrington.

support. With this backing, and that of the Scottish king, Cumin was able to secure Durham Castle and start the campaign to become bishop. This did not go well; he had some help from senior clergy, but others would not bow to his demands and wanted an election to select a bishop. In an attempt to defeat the opposition, he arranged for a letter endorsing his claim, supposedly, from the Pope to be delivered. This was a forgery, which when uncovered ruined his credibility and lost him the support of the Scottish king, and church authorities away from Durham ordered a proper election of a bishop. In 1143 William St Barbara was selected but Cumin still held Durham. Roger de Conyers was one of the local barons who had opposed Cumin and, aware that Cumin could strike against him, he had taken the precaution of having a motte-and-bailey castle built at his base in Bishopton, south of Durham. The newly elected bishop based himself at Bishopton and attempted to enter Durham, but his troops were forced back by Cumin's men. However, Cumin realised his position was tenuous, so he left Durham, took his followers to the church at Kirk Merrington and fortified it. Gathering his forces together with those of barons from Seaham and Brancepeth, Conyers besieged the church and Cumin capitulated.

30. All Saints, Lanchester

The Roman Dere Street ran from York to Corbridge and passed close to Lanchester, where a fort was built by the road. Later stonework from the fort was used as a fine source of building material and some was incorporated in the early twelfth-century All Saints Church at Lanchester. A major change to the church came in 1284 when Bishop Anthony Bek made this another of his collegiate churches. To accommodate the canons the church was extended, and the chancel had stalls for the cannons added. This was a large parish and the bishop had concluded there was enough income to support seven canons and a dean. To provide funds they were given estates within the parish. However, it seems that the clergy were happy to take the income from the lands that had been bestowed on them but not so concerned about their obligations, which included providing services in the three chapels spread around the parish. In 1378 and again later the bishop reported members of the clergy were absent and the church in a poor state of repair. Nevertheless, the college continued until, as a part of the Reformation, all of these colleges were closed. The valuable possessions of the collegiate church were taken by the Crown, amongst which were the tithes that had brought income for the canons.

Tithes were a tax of one-tenth of the produce, collected to support the parish. The confiscated tithes at Lanchester were then awarded to laymen, known as impropriators. In the hands of laymen, the tithes could be traded. It became the practice in some places for tithes to be paid in cash rather than produce and this was formalised in 1836 with the Tithe Commutation Act. Detailed listings were made of the land in parishes and the amount of tithe rent that would become payable and to whom it was to be paid. When the tithe apportionment schedules for Lanchester were produced in 1843 there were tithe payments allocated to a number of impropriators. In other parishes the tithes had been endowed to charitable institutions; at Kelloe it was split between the vicar, who received £19, and Sherburn hospital with £10 8*s* 4*d* (£10.42). By this time there was resentment

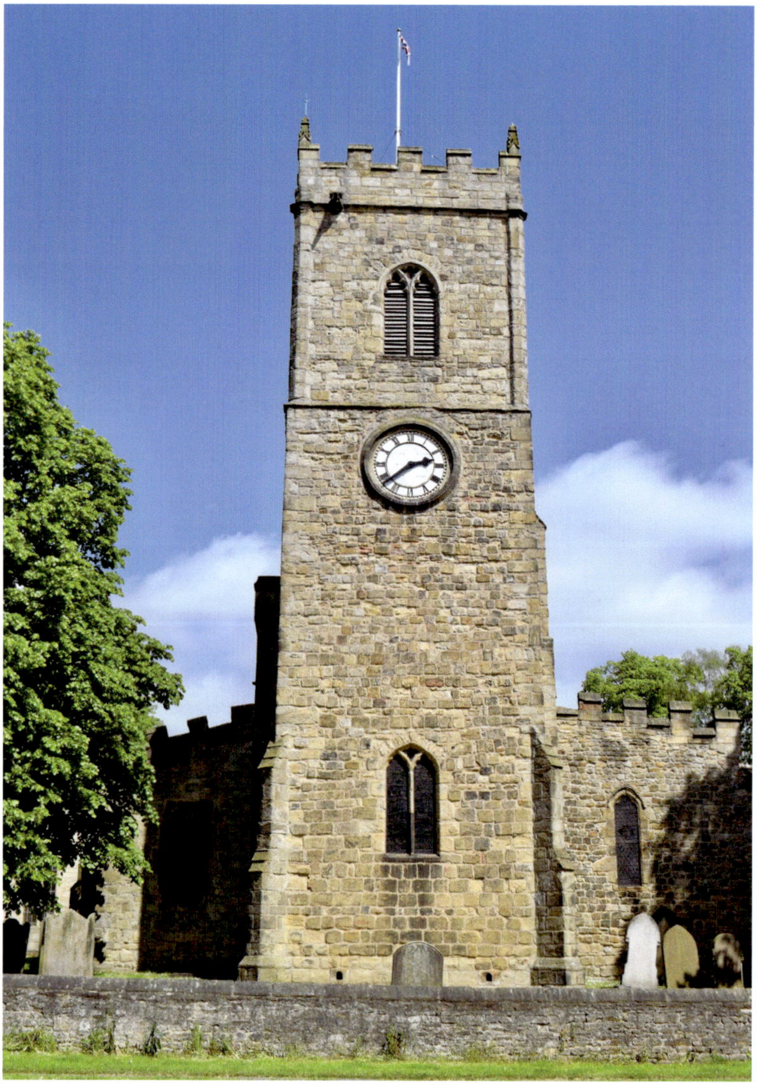

All Saints, Lanchester.

about the need to pay the tithe, and some expressed concern that whilst they were meant to support the church and the spread of religion, this was not achieved by paying impropriators. The Methodists, Baptists, Quakers, etc., had to support their own churches and meeting rooms and found it inequitable that they should also support the established church. Joseph Pease, a member of the Quaker family whose business interests extended to railways, coal and iron stone mines, textiles and banking, would clash with church authorities. In 1858 a summons against him for non-payment of church rates was dropped by the churchwardens of St Andrew in Bishop Auckland. This brought comments in a local newspaper that it was hoped the churchwardens 'could sustain the fabric of the church without seeking to compel those who do not worship there and have no sympathy with the place'.

31. St Mary the Virgin, Middleton-in-Teesdale

In 1877 the vicar of St Mary's was concerned about the state of repair of the church and was reported to have said that he would like to roll it into the River Tees. Less radical suggestions talked of renovation or rebuilding. There had been a church on the site since the twelfth century and the church the vicar was complaining about was from that era. Something had to be done and the decision was made to build a new church. By early 1878 builders were invited to provide quotations for the demolition of the old and the building of a new church. The cost was £4,500 and donations were needed to fund this. The largest was £2,000 from the Duke of Cleveland, but more money had to be raised. This was where the church bazaar came in. The stalls for one were set up in a venue provided by the London Lead Company (LLC) – often referred to as the Quaker Company because of its ownership. The LLC had become a major employer in the north Pennines in its lead mines and smelters. Middleton-in-Teesdale had been chosen for its headquarters with a grand administration building and, for the miners and

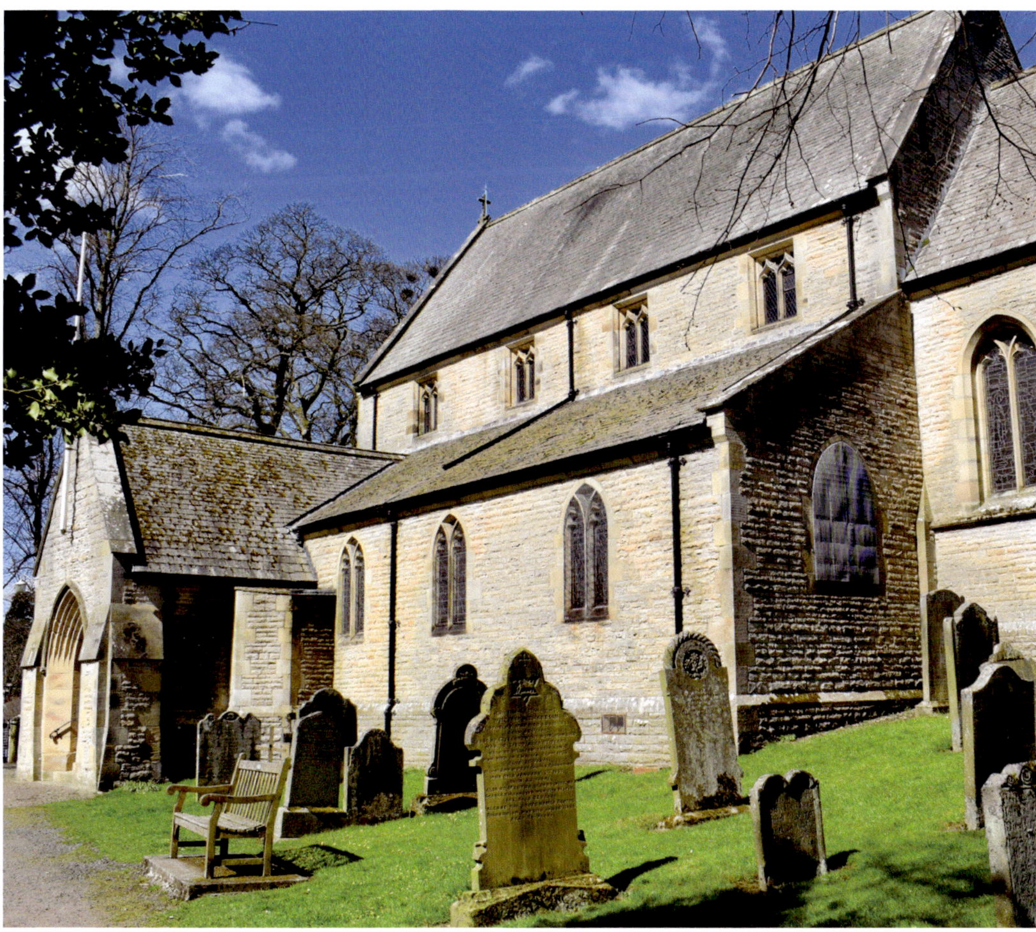

St Mary the Virgin, Middleton-in-Teesdale.

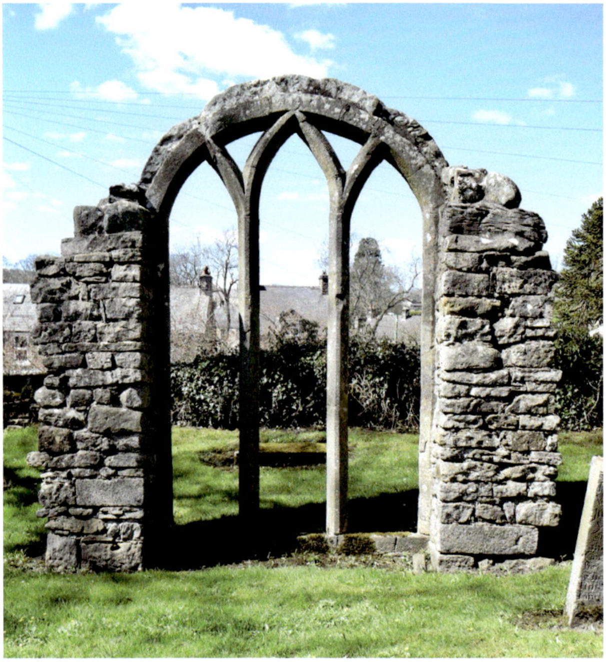

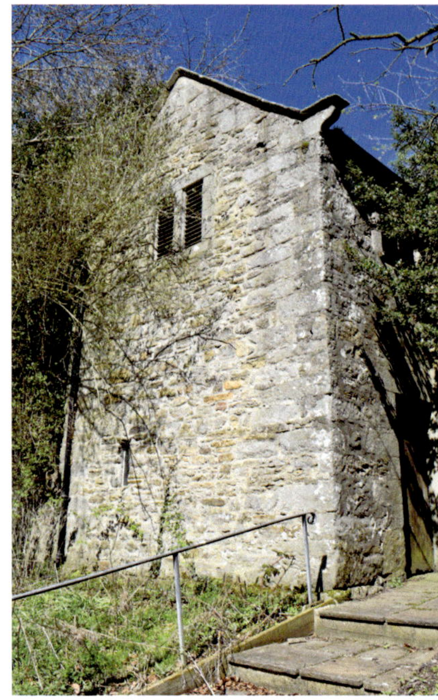

Above left: St Mary's Church in Middleton-in-Teesdale was rebuilt in the nineteenth century. Part of the earlier church has been kept in the churchyard.

Above right: The unusual belfry in Middleton-in-Teesdale stands alone away from the church.

their families, housing and a school in a part of the village that became known as Newtown.

The completed church was consecrated in 1879. Not everything of the old church was destroyed and part of it was left standing amongst the gravestones. Another reminder of the earlier church is the unusual belfry. It dates from the sixteenth century. It is isolated from the church, standing alone at the edge of the graveyard.

32. All Saints, Muggleswick

This must be one of the most isolated churches in the county. It is high in the moorland and once the surfaced road ends it is approached along a grassed track. It dates from the early nineteenth century, a replacement for the original thirteenth-century church. The village was the site of a monastic grange, which was a farming community that supplied food for the priors at Durham. Some of the buildings of the grange, which included a farm, hall and a chapel, survive.

Muggleswick gained notoriety after the Restoration of the Monarchy in 1660. The authority of the Church of England was confirmed and to ensure the supremacy of the Church of England a group of legislation known as the Clarendon Code was introduced. However, many dissenting groups, which had established themselves during the republic, felt aggrieved at being ignored and marginalised. This brought grumblings, which led to scheming to improve their position. One group of

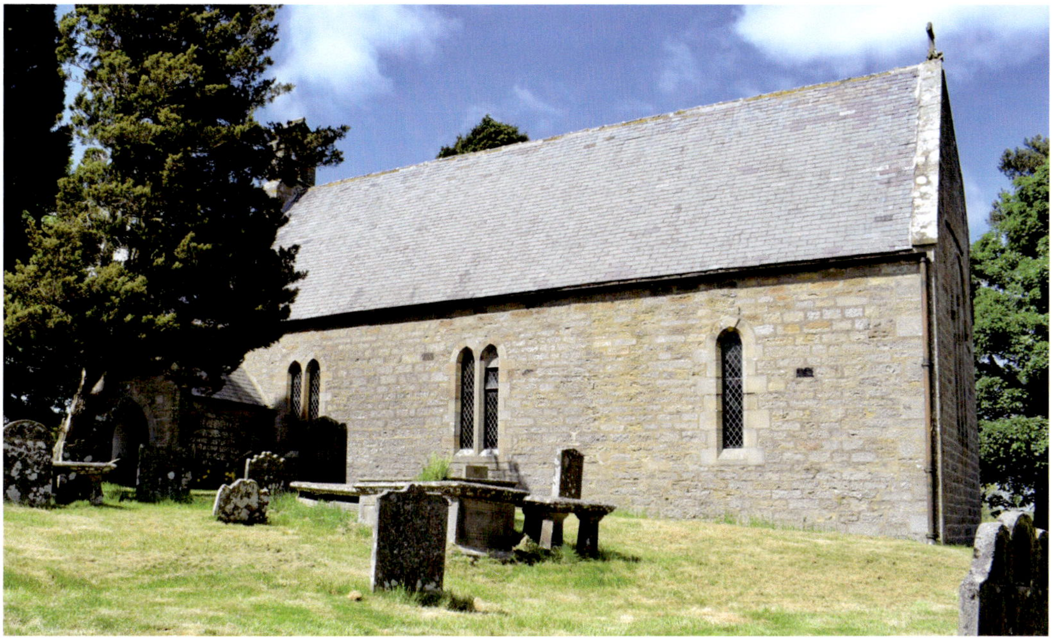

Above: The remote All Saints, Muggleswick.

Below: The remains of the chapel at Muggleswick, built when the estate was in the hands of the Priors of Durham.

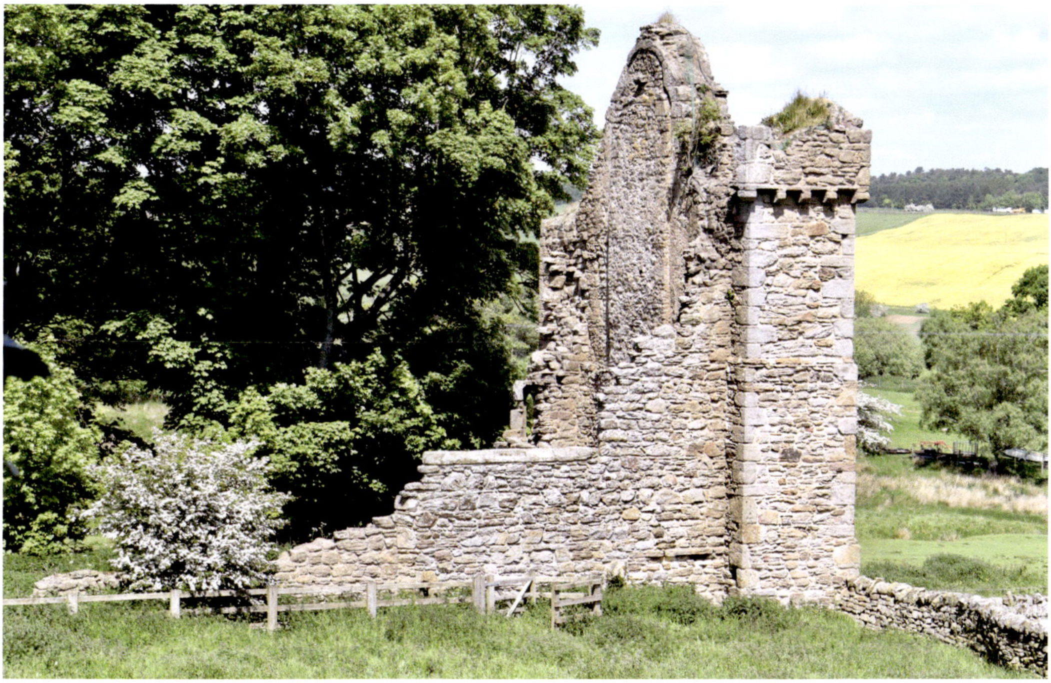

discontents met on Muggleswick in 1662. They plotted to take radical action and by 1663 had vowed to 'rise in rebellion against the government and murder all Bishops and Deans ... and all other ministers of the church ... and pull down all churches'. Among the group was John Etherington, whose conscience forced him to confess to Durham's Bishop Cosin, who acted, and arrests were made. The uncovering of this plot confirmed the fears that dissatisfaction amongst members of the dissenting groups could become a serious threat to maintaining stability, and there was real concern about the potential for disturbances. King Charles II became aware of the plot and in 1664 referred in parliament to 'the recent treason in the North' and went on to warn 'we are not at the bottom of this yet'. There were other groups around the country with the same purpose, meeting in secrecy to plan uprisings. However, the authorities were now forewarned and were able to infiltrate some groups and build a network of informers. Arrests were made before plans could be carried out. More legislation followed under the banner of the Clarendon Code including the Convective Act of 1664, which outlawed religious meetings of more than five people that were not under the auspice of the Church of England.

33. Methodist Chapel, Newbiggin

During the second half of the eighteenth century the Methodist movement became established across the country. John Wesley with his brother Charles and George Whitfield were the founders of the movement and it was Whitfield who introduced John to preaching outdoors in town squares, by market crosses and in fields. The expanding lead mining operation in the remote north Pennines brought

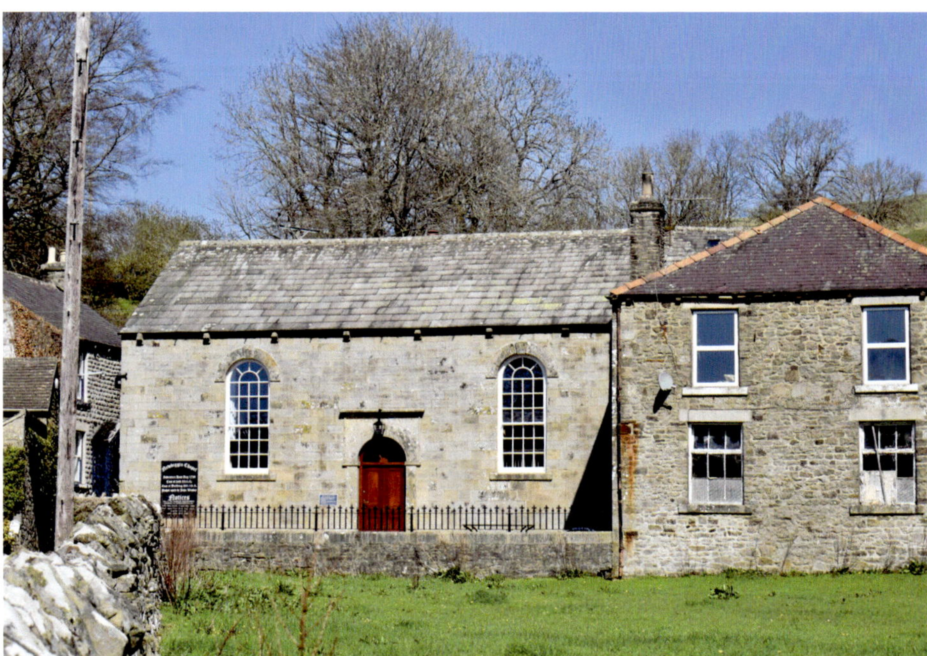

Methodist Chapel, Newbiggin.

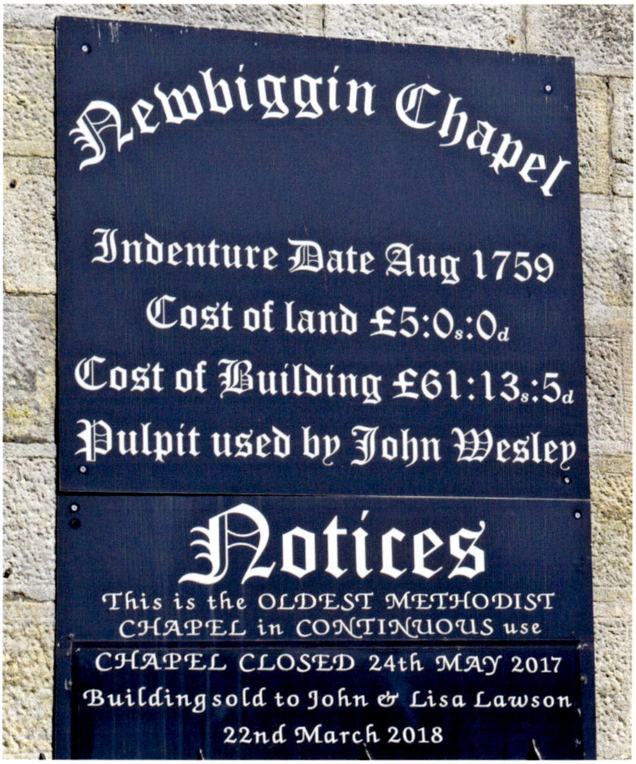

A brief history is displayed on the walls of Newbiggin chapel.

more people into the area and the Methodists were naturally attractive to those who did not want to travel to distant parish churches. Some of the earliest chapels built in County Durham were in these parts including the Newbiggin chapel, near Middleton-in-Teesdale, dating from 1759.

John Wesley was often in the area; in 1761 he recorded in his journal that he preached in Teesdale where, he noted, most of the men were lead miners. He was back in 1764 preaching to a congregation in Teesdale and Weardale. He was preaching in Newbiggin in 1780 and again in 1784 when, at the age of eighty-one, he noted in his journal that he 'rode through rain and wind to Newbiggin in Teesdale. Being but a poor horseman and having a rough horse, I had just strength for my journey … but after resting a while, I preached without any weariness'.

Whilst a plaque on the chapel wall tells that it was the oldest Methodist chapel in continuous use (1760–2017), it is a claim perhaps beaten by the Methodist High House Chapel at Ireshopeburn in Weardale, which was built in 1760 and used for services until 2019. The Newbiggin chapel was sold in 2018 and converted into holiday accommodation.

34. St Mary, Norton

How old is this ancient church, which stands beside the village green? It is a Grade I listed building, and the description of the listing tells that it provides the 'only evidence of a Saxon cross plan in County Durham'. It goes on to note

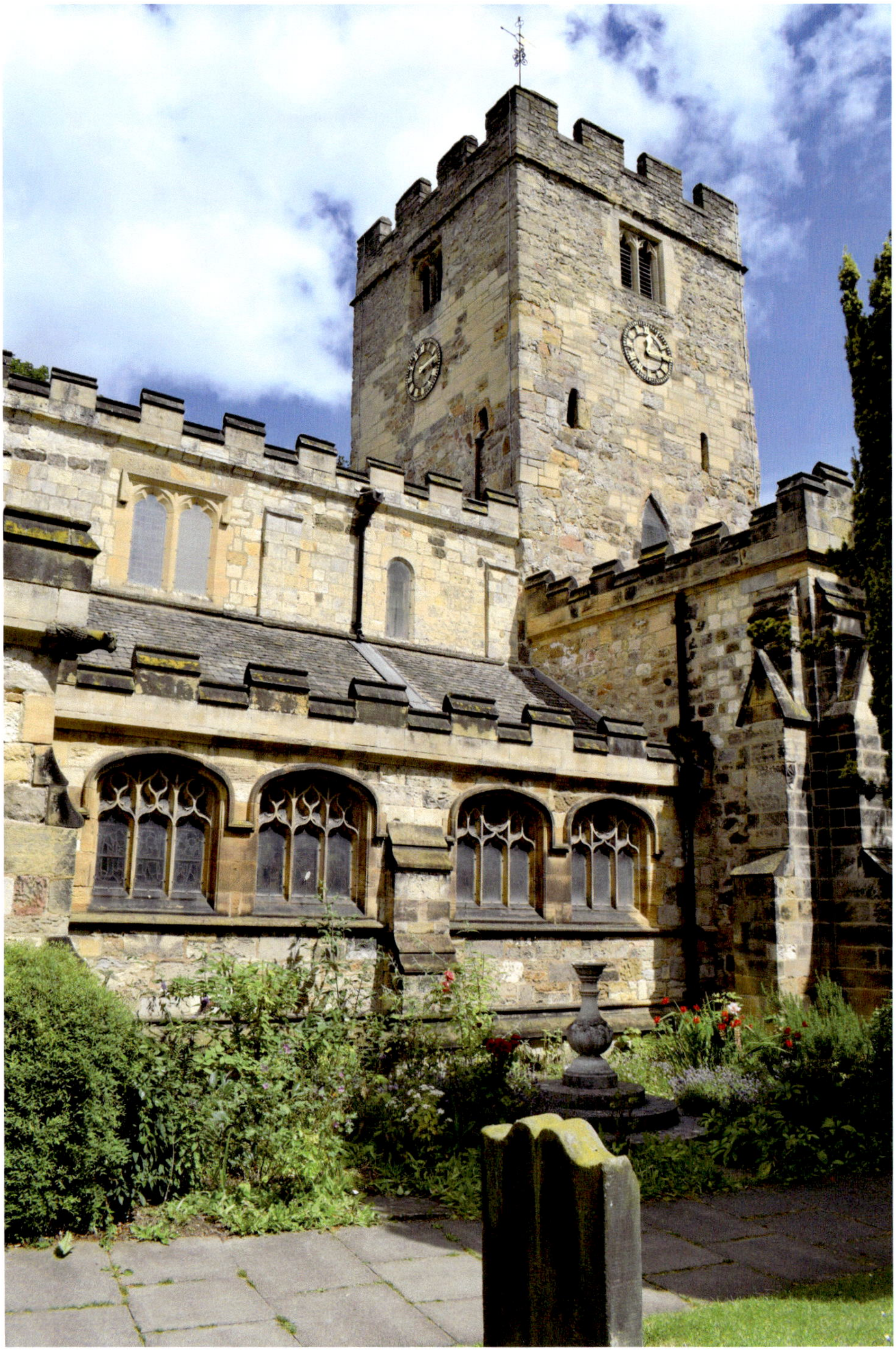

St Mary, Norton.

twelfth-, fifteenth- and nineteenth-century additions. However, there is some doubt raised about this Saxon label in Roberts, Pevsner and Williamson *The Buildings of England: County Durham*, where it is put as 'just into the Norman period'. Whilst there seems to be some uncertainty about its origin, there was a need to have a church by 1083 when it became another of the collegiate churches to accommodate the clergy who were removed from Durham when the cathedral became a Benedictine monastery.

After the Reformation and the closure of the collegiate churches, St Mary's continued as the church for the parish, which included Stockton-on-Tees. A Stockton man is remembered in the graveyard at Norton where his memorial records that 'John Walker chymist & druggist of Stockton on Tees who departed this life 1 May 1859 aged 78yrs. Highly respected by all who knew him ... The above John Walker was the original inventor of matches (friction lights)'. By 1827 John was selling friction matches from his shop in Stockton High Street, charging 1*s* (5p) for a box of a hundred. This was a breakthrough and a step to replacing the tinder box and the involved process of starting a fire.

35. Peter Lee Memorial Church, Peterlee

Along with Newton Aycliffe, and in the 1960s with Washington, Peterlee was one of the new towns developed in the county after the Second World War. The plain brick Peter Lee Methodist Church was opened in the town in 1958 and remembers the man the town is named after. Peter Lee was born in 1864 in Trimdon and started work when he was only ten, beginning a long connection with the mines. By the time he was sixteen he was looking for adventure and booked a passage to America. There he earned a living as a miner. He returned to England, married, fathered children and decided to leave his family behind and try his luck in South Africa, where, of course, he worked in mines. He was back home by 1897 working as a checkweighman. This was an important job; the miners relied on him to check the weight of coal brought to the surface and to ensure it was properly recorded as their wages depended on it.

His next move was into local politics, first as a member of Easington Rural District Council and in 1909 he was elected to Durham County Council. In 1919 he became the chairman of the first Labour led council and remained on the county council for twenty-six years. He was often involved in fighting for miners' rights including the long disputes after the First World War. The mines had been taken over by the government during the war, and when they were returned to the owners in March 1921 the post-war economic boom had ended and demand for coal, and consequently the price, was dropping. The mine owners, bearing in mind that the major cost of mining coal was wages, looked to reduce pay. The miners would not accept this and were locked out. At a shareholders' meeting in 1921 of Pease and Partners Ltd, which had extensive interest in collieries, Sir Arthur Pease explained that 'trading conditions were becoming difficult and if costs were not reduced ... problems would follow. Workmen should take lower wages now and employers take little or no profit'. Reduced profit was one thing, but Peter would not accept a reduction in wages to a level that would bring poverty. He demanded to know how a family survived at a time when the cost of food was rising, and

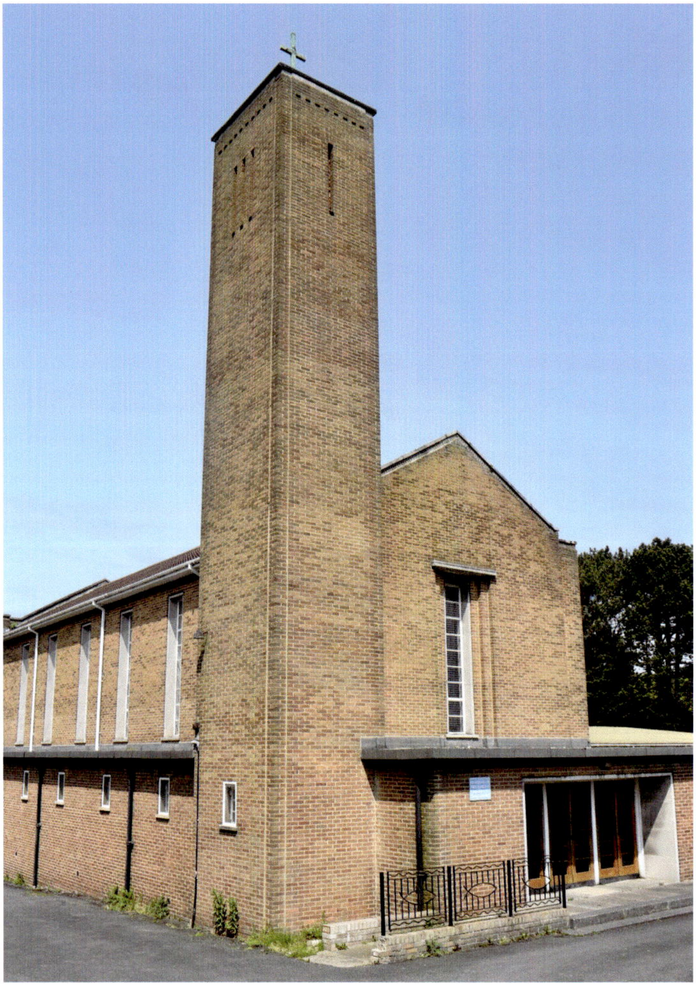

The plain, mid-twentieth-century Peter Lee Memorial Church, Peterlee.

no action was being taken by the government to control this. After three months the miners returned to work with reduced wages but the dispute rumbled on and another long strike followed in 1925. Peter continued to serve the miners: he was elected to positions in the miners' union first as General Secretary of Durham Miners Association, then he served as President of the National Miners Federation and still found time to be a Methodist preacher. Peter died in 1935.

36. St Laurence, Pittington

To the west of Durham is Hallgarth and the splendid church dedicated to St Laurence. The church was, until dissolution, within Hallgarth Manor, which was one of the estates owned by the Prior of Durham at the monastery at Durham Cathedral. It was centred around a manor house and farm buildings. By the nineteenth century the nearby villages of High and Low Pittington provided a boost to the congregation when coal mines were opened. This was

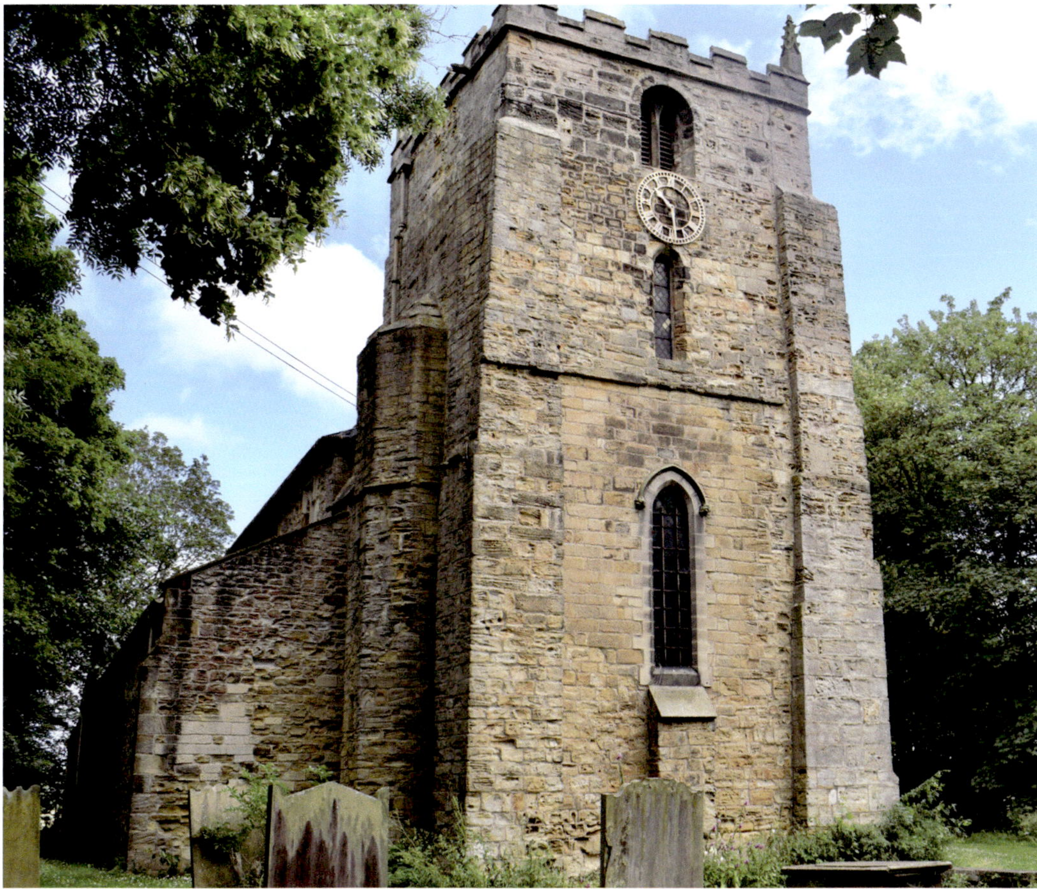

Above: St Laurence, Pittington.

Right: Wall paintings at St Laurence, Pittington, depicting St Cuthbert.

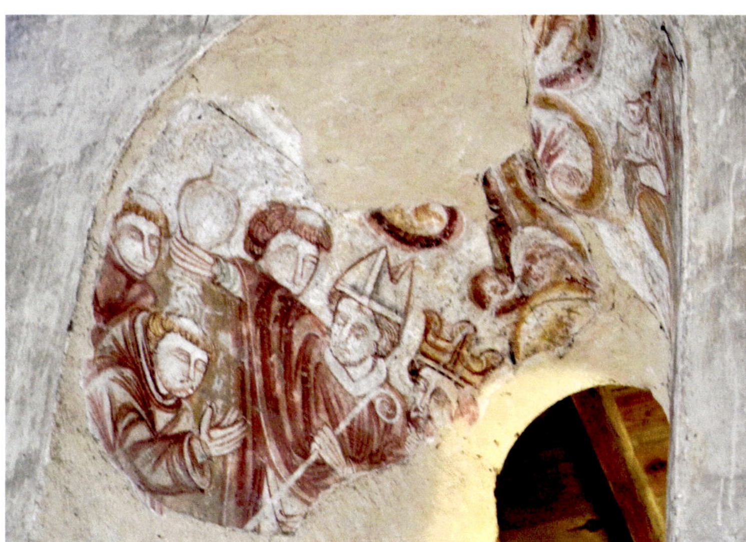

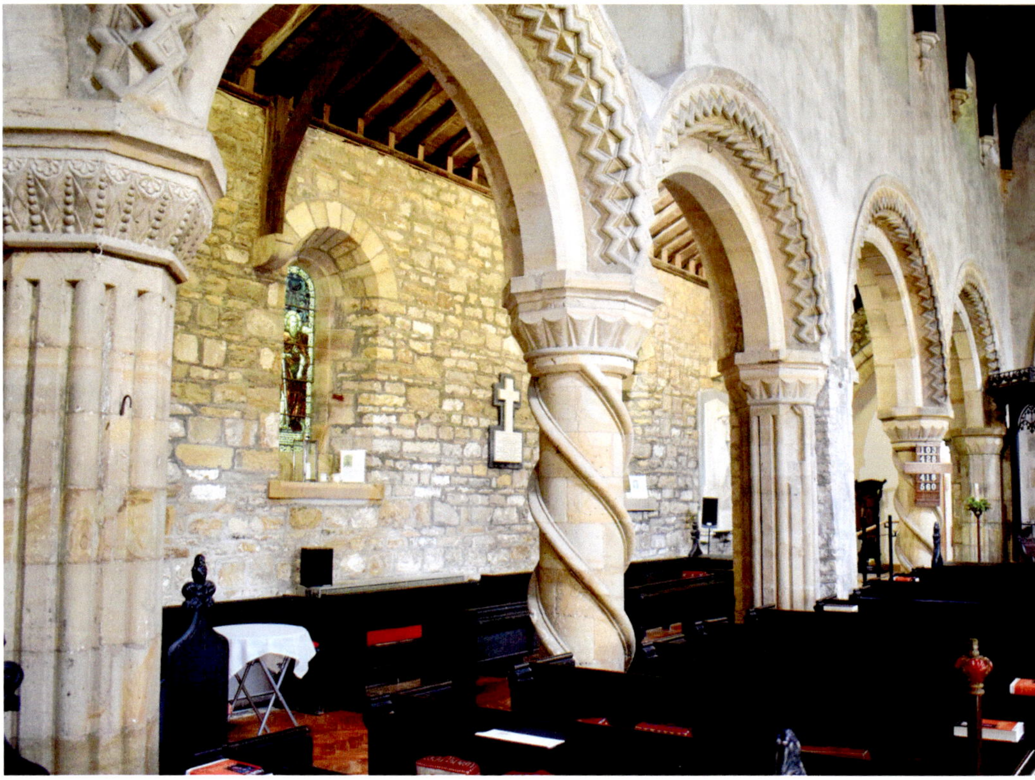

The grand Norman arcade at Pittington.

the time when renovation work was undertaken by Ignatius Bonami, who was wise enough to retain much of the early architecture. This included the northern arcade in the nave, which had been fashioned when the church was extended, and the aisle added in the medieval period, and is one of the finest features in this medieval church. The piers, some carved with spiral design, hold the rounded arches, which are intricately decorated with chevrons. Above the arches are narrow window openings from the early Norman church. One of the windows has the remains of wall paintings. These depict scenes from the life of St Cuthbert and date from the twelfth century. No doubt this was a useful way to relate the story of the saint in the days when many were illiterate. There is also a memorial to Christian, and it has been suggested that this could be recognising the mason who was employed by Bishop de Puiset and whose work is seen on the northern aisle.

37. St Helen, St Helens Auckland

An early Norman church, extended over the centuries and much improved in 2001 with an extensive renovation, the original door has been retained and is described as one of the oldest in the country. The porch is unusual with two storeys, the upper one built as a priest's room.

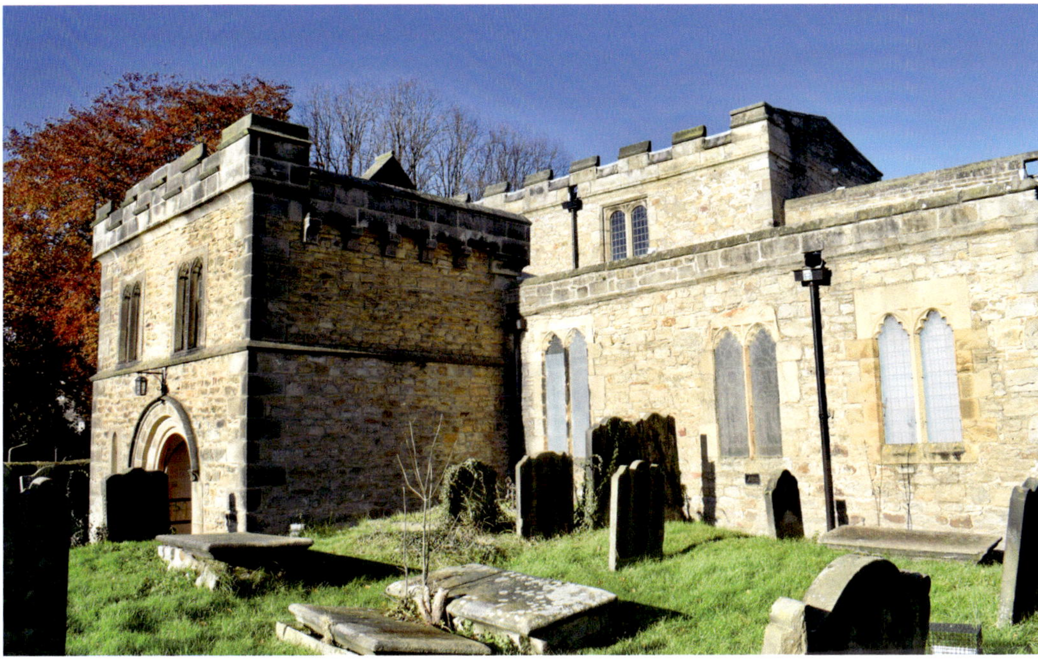

St Helen, St Helen Auckland.

John Vaux was the vicar at the church in 1633. He was depicted as a rascal when he was in front of the church authorities charged with many misdemeanours. His crimes included selling his almanac from the communion table. He published this every year with astronomical charts and predictions for the year ahead. Witnesses were called to recount his irregular behaviour and some told that he was often in the 'ale house' on Sunday, while others told of his reputation for having the power to see what had happened to lost or stolen property and charging for this service. One incident told of a lost horse. The owner had heard of John's powers and sought his help. John could only say the animal had strayed and it would return. The horse did not find its way back and more consultations followed until John was able to give the name of the man who had the horse. On another occasion he told an owner that his horses had gone towards Stainmore. (How involved was he in these disappearances?) His punishment was a suspension of three years from his church duties and imprisonment for a year.

38. St Mary, Seaham

Standing above the cliffs overlooking the sea is St Mary's Church at Seaham. Close by is Greystones, built around 1830 as the vicarage but has now been converted into private residences. A plaque on the boundary wall of St Mary's tells that this is an ancient church dating back to the seventh or eighth century. The Saxon heritage is suggested by the small narrow windows in the nave, which are typical of Saxon churches, although, like other churches, it could incorporate some Saxon building techniques as these continued in use into the early years of

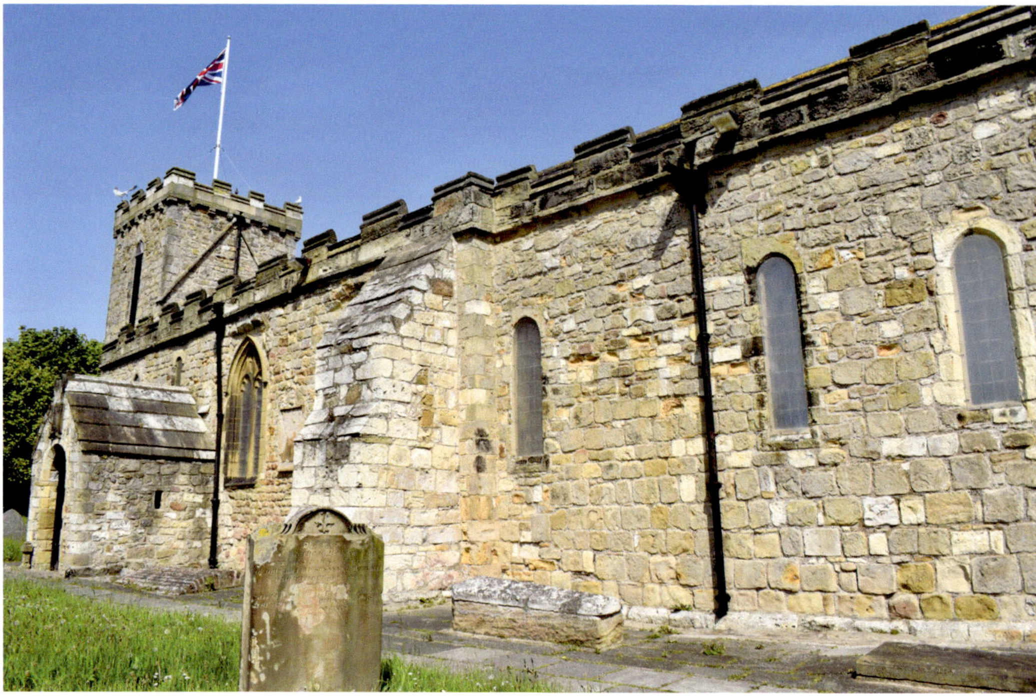

Above: St Mary, Seaham.

Below: Once the grand vicarage attached to St Mary, Seaham, now private accommodation.

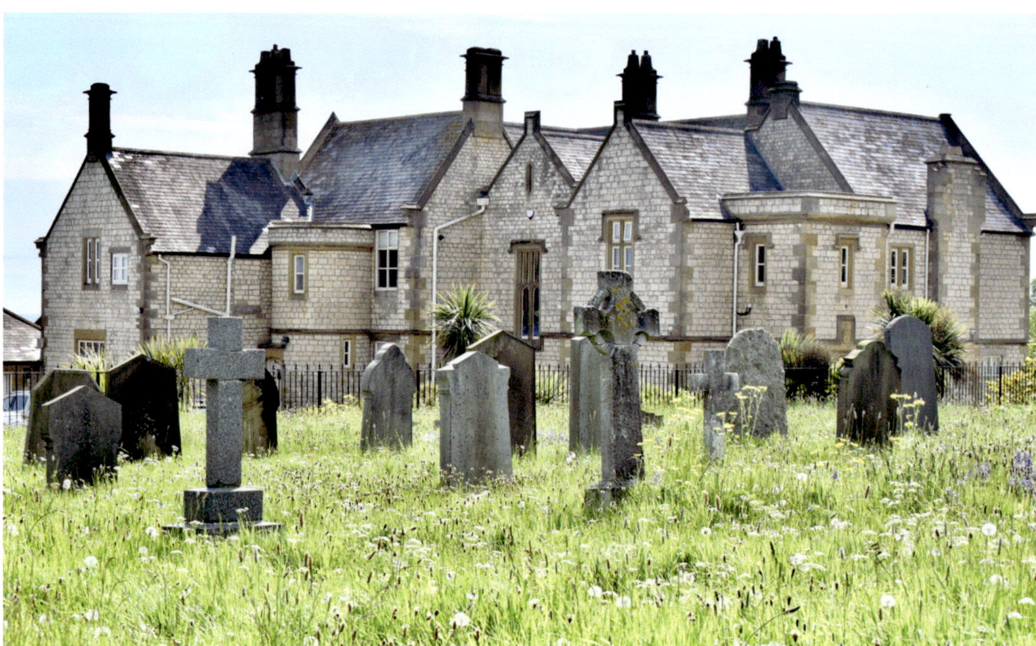

the Norman era. Nevertheless, there was an ancient settlement in the area, and a cemetery with burials dating from the seventh century has been found near the church. In 934 King Athelstan gave land at Seaham to the community of monks who had left Lindisfarne because of the constant threat of Viking raids and taken the remains of St Cuthbert to Chester-le-Street. Athelstan, the grandson of Alfred the Great, is credited as being the first king of a united country. The Seaham estate passed through many owners until 1821 when it was bought by the Marquess of Londonderry, by which time the village was little more than a farming community, dominated by Seaham Hall and the church.

39. St John the Evangelist, Seaham Harbour

When the Marquess of Londonderry bought the Seaham estate, he developed the plan formulated by the previous owner to build a port from which coal could be shipped. The port was opened in 1831 and coal was brought by a new railway connected to the Londonderry pit at Rainton. Soon Seaham harbour was becoming a busy industrial centre, and more coal was brought to the docks from another mine sunk nearby at New Seaham. Around the port bottle works were opened, as well as, in 1859, blast furnaces to produce iron. Seaham harbour was developing, and churches were needed amongst the growing town. The Methodists were the first with two chapels, Wesleyan and United Methodist. The foundation stone for St John's Church was laid by Frances

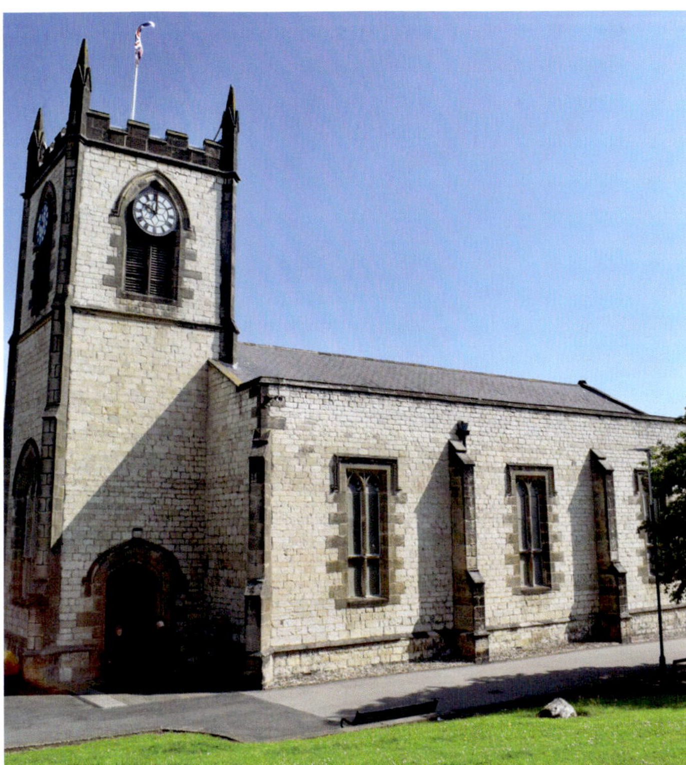

St John the Evangelist, Seaham harbour.

the Marchioness of Londonderry in 1835 and consecrated in 1840. The new parish of Seaham harbour was formed in 1845. One of the early incumbents at St John's was Angus Bethune, who was actively involved in the national school and the local hospital. He also became a magistrate. One case he heard involved two overzealous policemen, who were asked to remove some men who were arguing in a pub. They went too far and threw everybody out of the pub and, in doing so, used a truncheon on a seventy-year-old man, knocking him to the floor and kicking him. The two were brought in front of Angus, who found they had exceeded their duty and fined them £3 each; the Chief Constable was even harder and sacked them.

40. St Edmund, Sedgefield

St Edmund's is another church with a long history. Building started in 1246, although there was probably an earlier church on the site. The transepts and chancel were added later in the century and, later still, the tower. Bishop Cosin had the choir stalls built in the seventeenth century. In the south transept there are two recesses with effigies, one of a man, but time has left few features recognisable.

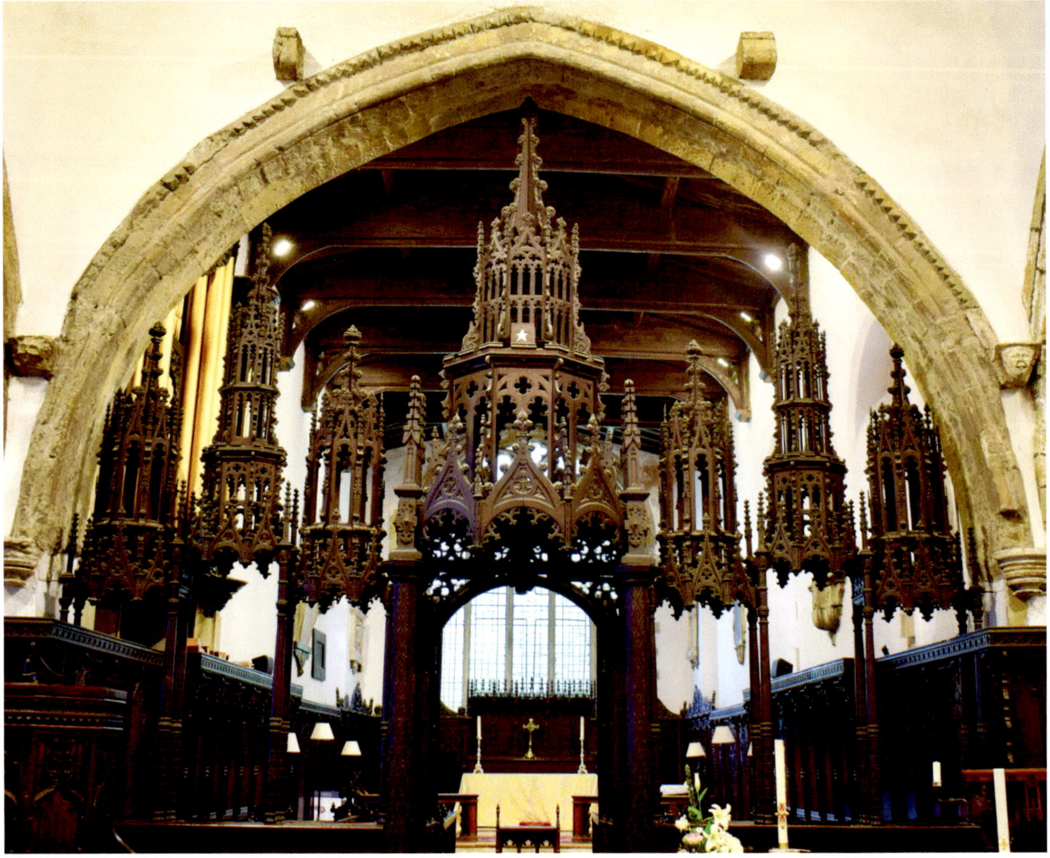

The interictally decorated chancel screen inside St Edmund, Sedgefield.

The other is a lady in a wimple. Similarly dressed is another lady, this time portrayed in one of the brasses in the church, which is dated to around 1390. Another brass from the sixteenth century depicts the skeletons of a man and a woman – perhaps a reminder of the fate of us all.

After Henry VIII's break with Rome many in the county remained loyal to the Catholic faith and the Northern Rebellion of 1569 gave the opportunity to show their allegiance in public. In Sedgefield, the news of the rebellion brought the villagers to the church to hear mass given by the rector Richard Hartborn. A fire was started at the edge of town and the Protestant bibles, psalm book and sermons were torn up and burnt. This was not an isolated incident and it would seem that away from the forces that were taking part in the rebellion there was a desire to be rid of the religion imposed by the state. For the authorities, these local shows of support for the old religion helped to reinforce the idea that Catholics were potential traitors and had to be guarded against.

Later a legend developed around another incumbent, John Gamage, who, when he died in 1747, left his wife with a dilemma. She knew that on his death the

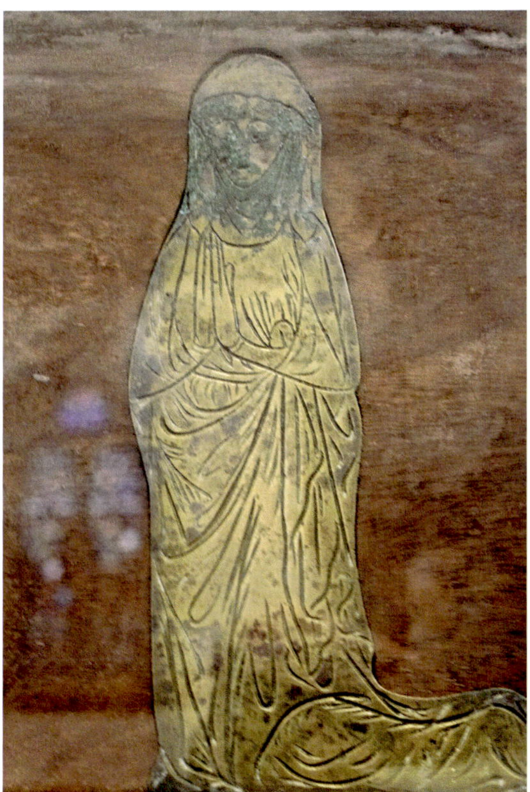

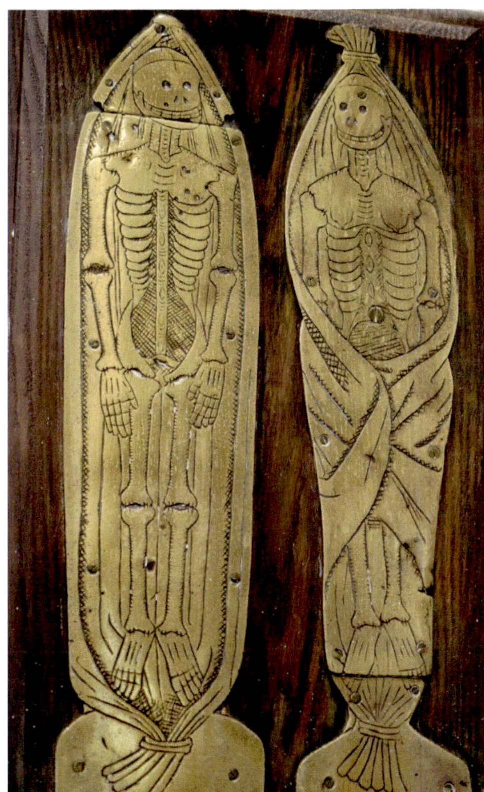

Above left: One of the treasures at St Edmund, Sedgefield, is this early brass dated to 1310.

Above right: Another set of brasses at Sedgefield's church, this time of skeletons wrapped in shrouds.

income from the tithes, which were almost due to be collected, would go to the bishop. To survive and feed her children she needed the funds, so she decided to preserve his body by pickling him and on the day the tithes were paid she propped him in a chair beside a window, so he was in full view of parishioners, who called and paid his wife. Needless to say, the vicarage was haunted by the pickled parson for years.

41. St John, Shildon

Coal had been mined in County Durham for centuries. As far back as 1183 the Boldon Book mentions at Escomb a collier who held 'one toft and one croft and finds coals for making the iron work of the ploughs at Coundon'. In the south of the county coal mining had remained at a relatively low level while in the north of the county the coal trade was well developed. By the start of the nineteenth century a network of tramways was being used to take coal to be loaded onto ships docked on the Tyne and Wear ready for export, mainly to London. Further south the cost of transporting coal restricted the development of mines. That was until the opening of the Stockton & Darlington Railway in 1825. Freight charges were drastically cut, and coal mining became an attractive business, changing the fortunes of the area. The railway started the development of Shildon as a railway town, which gathered momentum when Timothy Hackworth set up locomotive

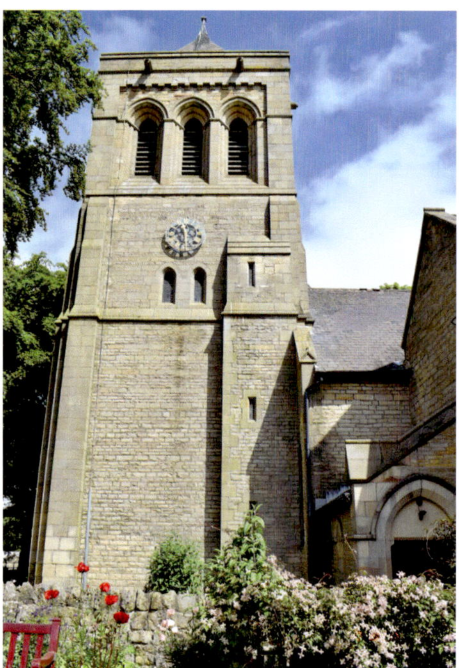

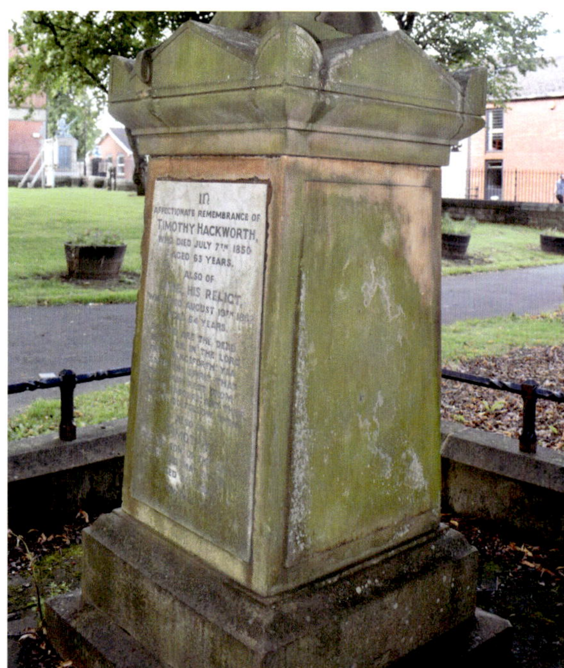

Above left: St John, Shildon.

Above right: Within the grounds of St John's Church at Shildon is this memorial to Timothy Hackworth.

workshops in the area that became New Shildon. This new settlement had no church. However, the original Shildon village was expanding with work available on railways, as well as in the newly opened pits, and so St John's Church was opened. The church was built in 1831 but within half a century had become too small, and it was also in poor repair, being described as very damp and miserable. Renovation was carried out; walls were replaced, and the newly extended church was reopened in 1882. By the churchyard is a monument remembering Timothy Hackworth. In New Shildon churches took a little longer to arrive with the Wesleyan Methodists in 1865 and All Saints in 1868, although they do not survive as places of worship.

42. All Saints, Sockburn

To the south of the ancient county the River Tees meanders its way towards the sea and forms a peninsular that holds the ruined church at Sockburn. This was an early religious site of some importance, and as far back as the eighth century it is said that Higbald was crowned here as Bishop of Lindisfarne. The pre-Conquest church was expanded in the thirteenth century and the Conyers chapel was added in the next century.

The story of the Sockburn Worm introduces the Conyers family, who became major landowners in the area, and acclaimed for the slaying of the Sockburn worm. The Lampton worm is perhaps a more celebrated legend in the county, commemorated with the Penshaw Monument on the hill that the worm was said to wrap itself around ten times. Equally fearsome was the venomous, fire-breathing monster at Sockburn and it was left to Sir John Conyers to act and free the neighbourhood of the terrifying dragon. Ready to face the beast he donned his armour and, taking his sword, spent the night praying in the church. Good triumphed over evil and Sir John killed and sliced the dragon before he buried it under the grey stone near the church. Quite what the story of the dragon was supposed to portray has led to many suggestions including a victory over Viking raiders, but the timing is wrong as the Conyers family were at Sockburn centuries after the Viking raids. Other suggestions look to wildlife, perhaps a giant eel lurking in the river or fierce bear roaming the countryside.

The Conyers Falchion, or sword, which plays its part in the dragon tale, is preserved in Durham Cathedral and was part of a ceremony used when a new Bishop of Durham entered the county. On the bishop's first arrival the Sockburn lord greeted the bishop with 'My Lord Bishop, I here present you with the falchion wherewith the champion Conyers slew the worm, dragon, or fiery flying serpent, which destroyed man, woman and child; in memory of which, the king then reigning gave him the manor of Sockburn, to hold by this tenure, that upon the first entrance of every Bishop into the county, this falchion should be presented'. The Tees was crossed by a ford at Neasham, then later by the drier route over the bridge at Croft. The ritual lapsed but was revived in 1984.

Lewis Carroll's father was the vicar at the church in nearby Croft between 1848 and 1868. Lewis would no doubt have been aware of the local folklore, and it has been suggested that his poem about the Jabberwocky, featured in his story

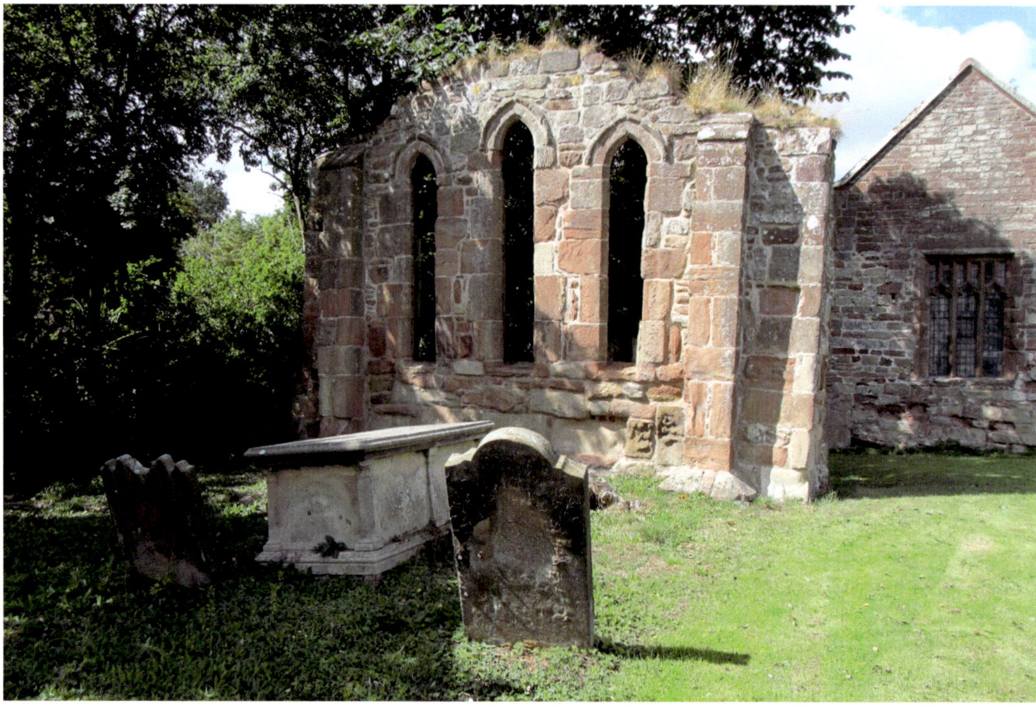

Above: All Saints, Sockburn.

Below: The Sockburn Falchion.

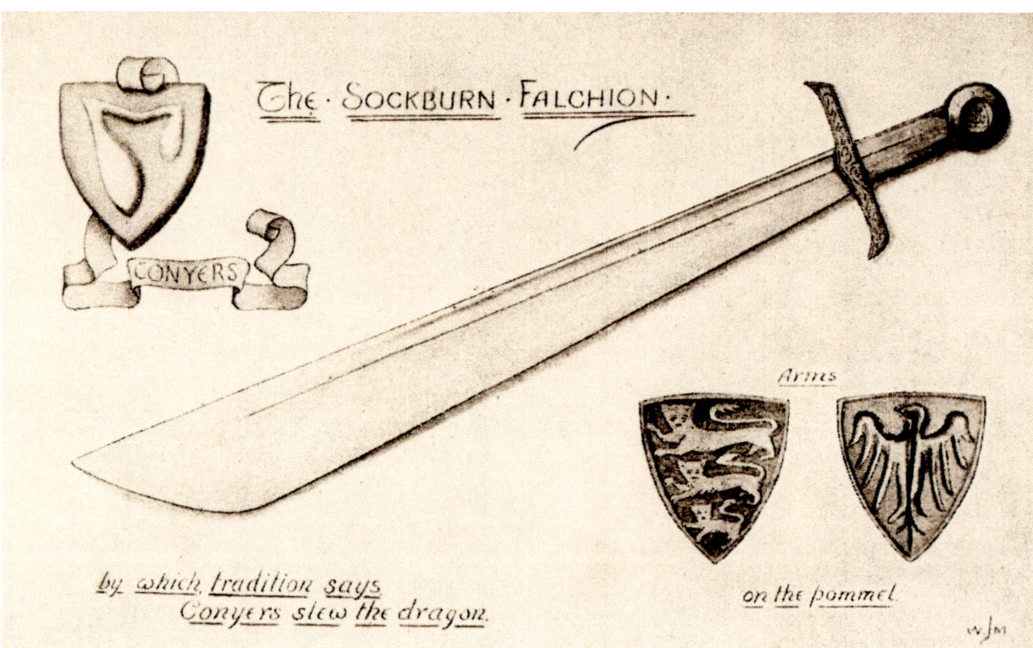

of Alice's adventures *Through the Looking Glass*, has roots in the slaying of the Sockburn dragon:

> One, two! One, two! And through and through
> The vorpal blade went snicker-snack!
> He left it dead, and with its head.
> He went galumphing back.

The church was dismantled in 1838 by the owner of the recently built Sockburn Hall and parishioners had to use the new church at Girsby. The Conyers Chapel was rescued, a new roof added, and it now stands with the remains of the ancient church.

43. St Mary's, Staindrop

A medieval church associated with kings, bishops and nobles. It is another site where there was probably an earlier church in the days when Canute was King of England between 1016 and 1035. Canute was Danish and took the throne after years of raids by Danish armies, culminating in a battle in 1016 where Canute defeated the English ruler, Edmund. Canute recognised the strength of Christianity in the country and, amongst his acts to ensure an alliance with the church, he donated the manor of Staindrop to the monks at Durham. Later it was in the hands of the Neville family, who became Earls of Westmorland and were based at the nearby Raby Castle. Inside the church are effigies in memory of family members. The extended south aisle has the tomb of Euphemia de Clavering, mother of

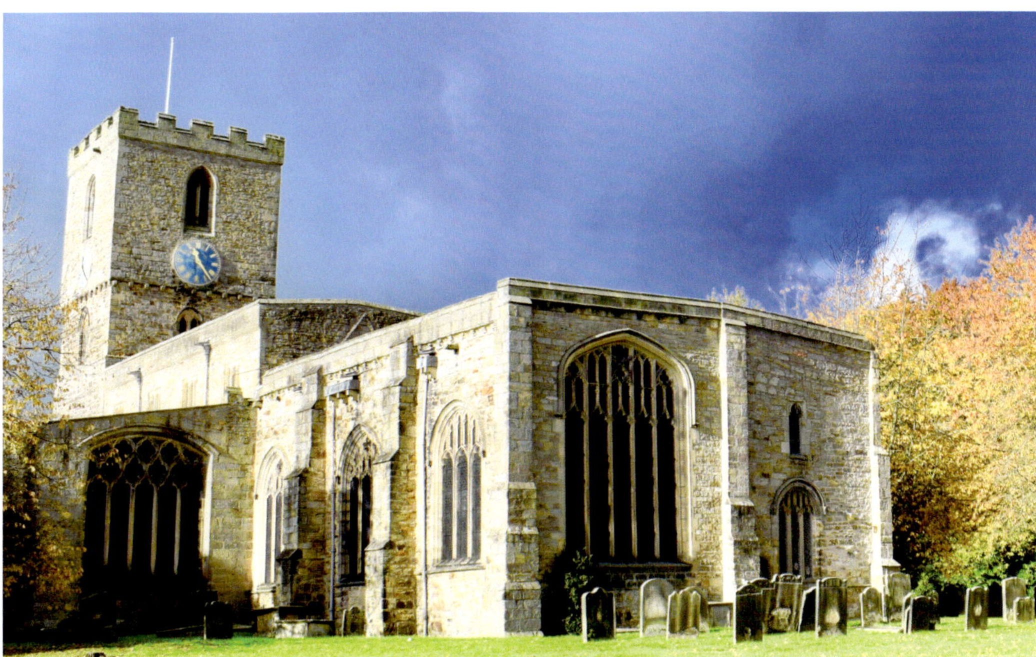

St Mary's, Staindrop.

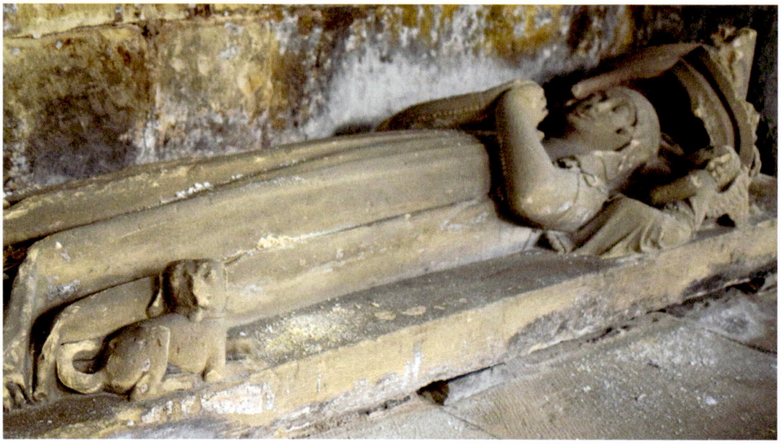

Left: The effigy of Euphemia de Clavering and her dog at Staindrop.

Below: This screen at St Mary's in Staindrop is one of the oldest screens to be found in the county's churches – early fifteenth century.

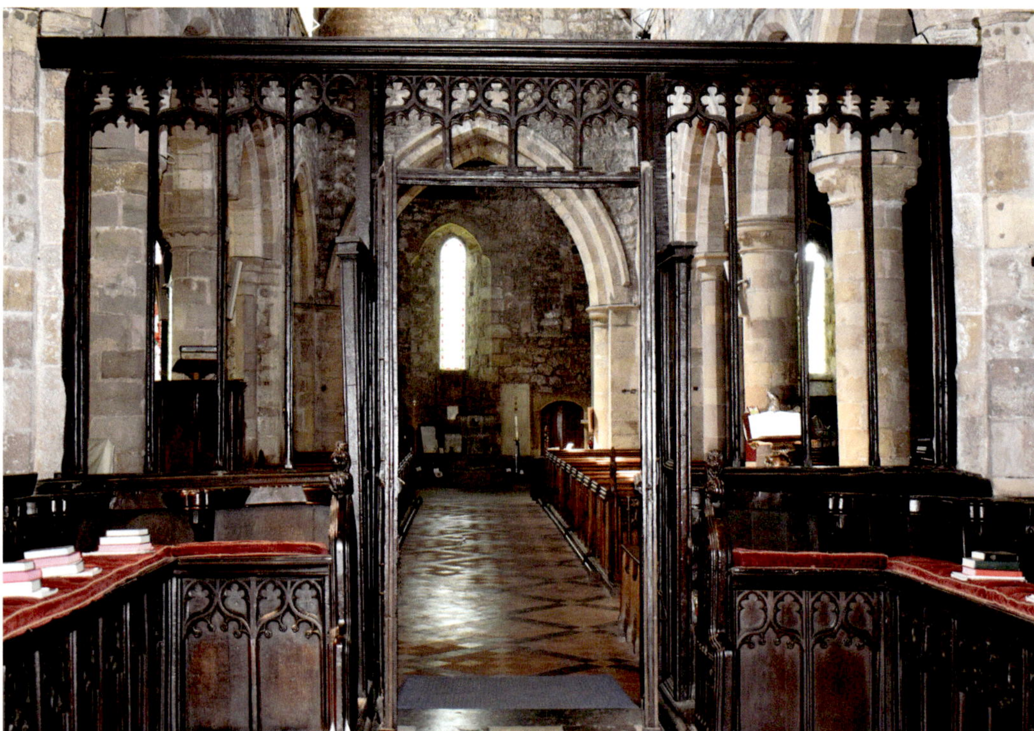

Ralph Neville, who led the English army to victory over Scottish invaders at the Battle of Neville's Cross in 1346. Near the entrance an effigy of Ralph's grandson, another Ralph, with his two wives, Joan Beaufort and Margaret Stafford, who between then produced twenty-two children. The south aisle was also the site of a three chantries colleges. Chantries were funded by endowments left to pay a priest to pray for a speedy deliverance through purgatory – a place of punishment where sins were cleansed before heaven could be entered.

The Neville's religious beliefs (see St Brandon at Brancepeth) would bring devastating setbacks to their prosperity and standing when their lands were confiscated by the crown. Sir Henry Vane, whose descendants would become the Earls of Darlington and the Dukes of Cleveland, bought the Raby estate. The church at Staindrop turned from a mausoleum to the Neville family to one for the Vanes.

44. St Thomas the Apostle, Stanhope

A twelfth-century church set in this market town at the edge of the Pennines. The church at Stanhope was in a wealthy parish which benefited from income from the lead mines in the area. The incumbents enjoyed a rich living, and two of those would go onto greater things. After leaving Stanhope, Cuthbert Tunstall became a diplomat working for Henry VIII before being appointed Bishop of Durham where his reticence to accept the move from Rome, which the Reformation brought, would be his downfall. His Catholic roots meant he could not fully support Henry and he had to tread a delicate path to avoid any recriminations. However, he could not accept the continuing reforms to church life that Henry's successor introduced and this, coupled with an accusation that he had some involvement in the Pilgrimage of Grace, the uprising in 1536 against the drastic changes to the traditional religion, led to his arrest. He was imprisoned in the Tower of London and the lost his position as bishop. Queen Mary, a Catholic, worked to restore the historic link with Rome and reversed much of the legislation previously enacted. She reinstalled Tunstall as Durham's

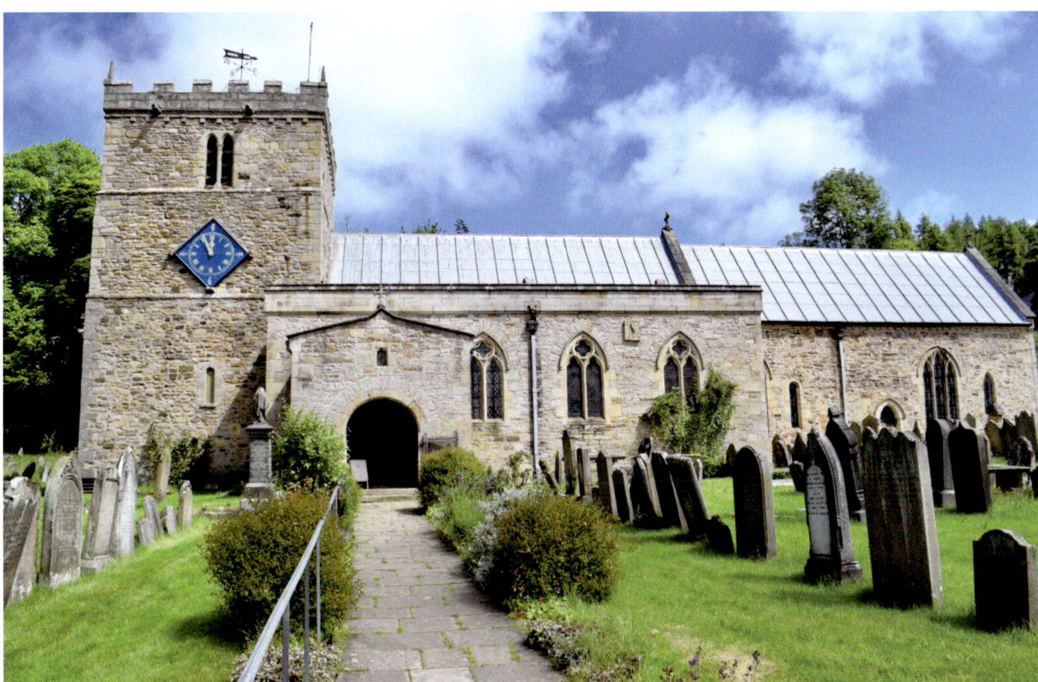

St Thomas the Apostle, Stanhope.

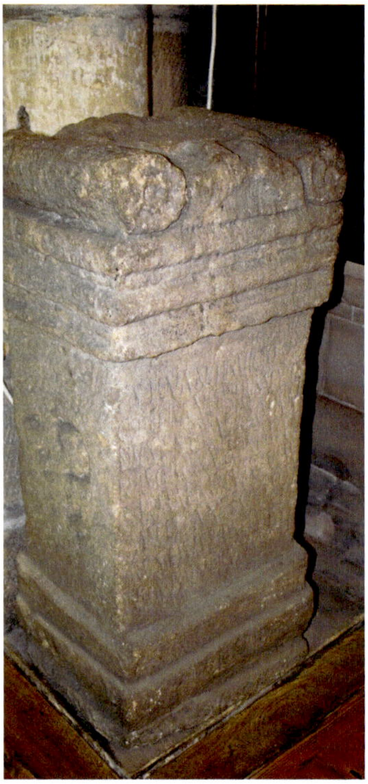

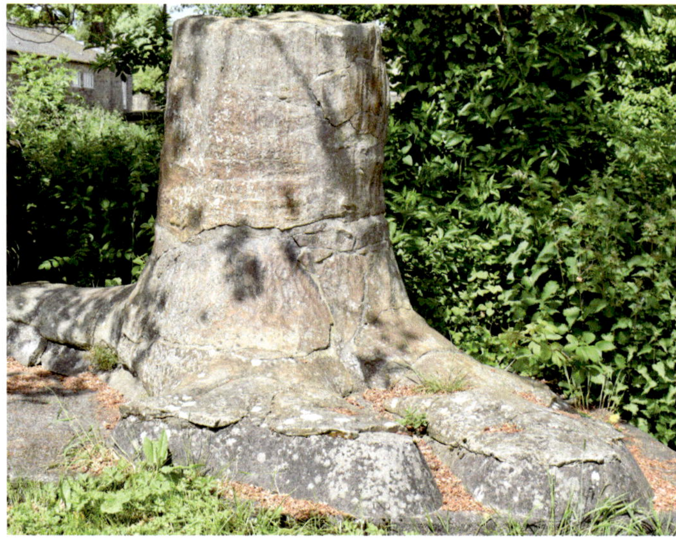

Left: The Roman alter on display inside Stanhope church.

Above: The fossilised tree at the edge of the grounds of St Thomas, Stanhope.

bishop but this was not to last. Tunstall lost his position again when Elizabeth became queen in 1558. She was a Protestant and started to overturn much of Mary's move towards Catholicism. Like all those in public or religious office, Tunstall was required to take the Oath of Supremacy that swore allegiance to the queen as supreme head of the English Church. Tunstall was not willing to take the oath. He was by this time eighty-five years old and, despite his age, he was arrested only to die a few weeks later in captivity. In 1725 Joseph Butler was at Stanhope and from there he went on to become chaplain to George II's wife, Queen Caroline, eventually returning to the area as Bishop of Durham.

Inside the church there is a font thought to be Anglo-Saxon. There is also a Roman alter, found nearby. The inscription tells that the alter is dedicated to Silvanus, the Roman god of woodland, and recognised the efforts of a soldier in hunting down a wild boar that had managed to escape the attempts of others to slaughter it. However, these ancient relics cannot match the age of the fossilised remains of part of a 250-million-year-old tree in the church grounds. This was uncovered in a local quarry in the early twentieth century and placed at the edge of the church grounds in the 1960s.

45. St Andrew, and St Joseph, Stanley

Two churches in Stanley were built to serve the growing mining community in the town, which until the nineteenth century was no more than a hamlet before the opening of mines brought drastic change. Pits were operated around

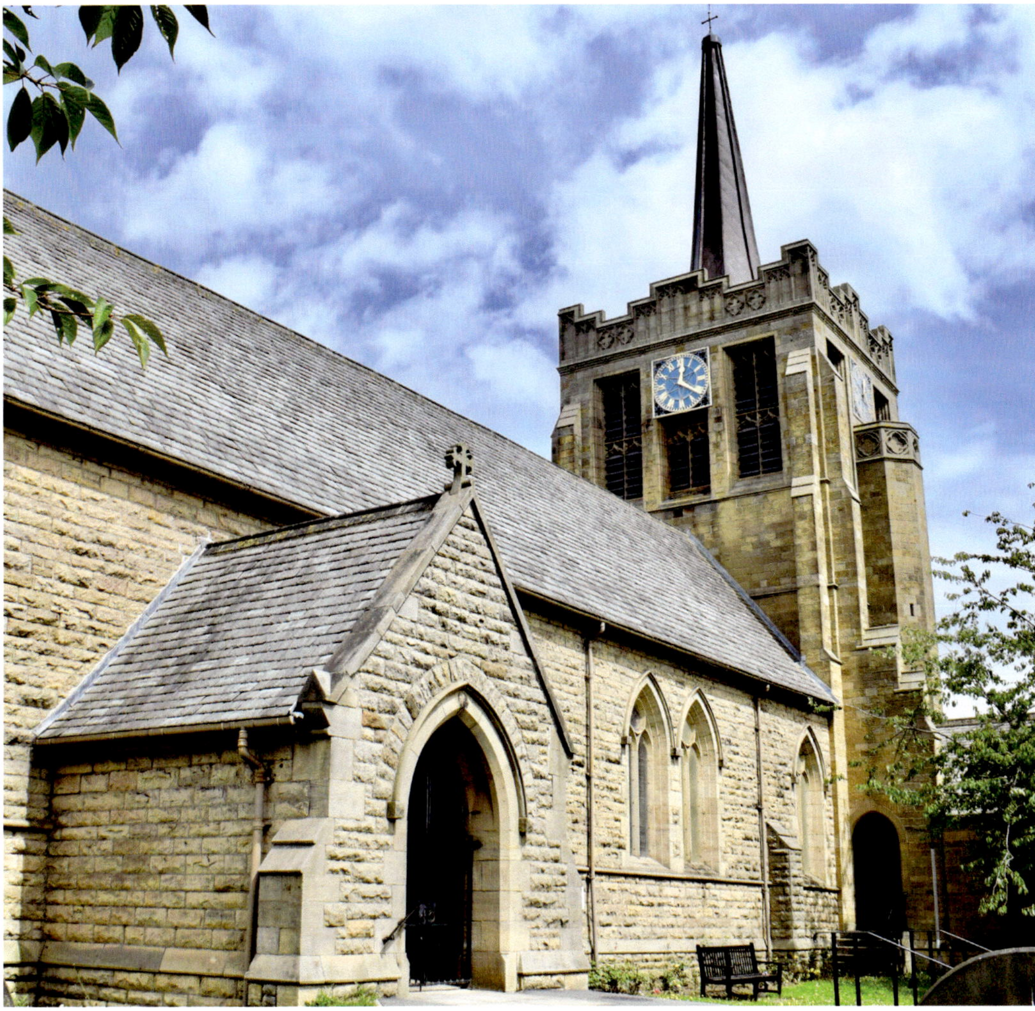

St Andrew, Stanley.

Stanley: the West Stanley pit was sunk in 1832 and at the other side of town there was the East Stanley pit. Eventually these two outpost settlements of the village would grow and merge to become part of Stanley. St Andrew's Church was built in 1876. St Joseph's Catholic Church followed in 1902, although it did suffer from a problem with subsidence from the mining work. In February 1909, the West Stanley pit was the site of one of the county's worst mining disasters. In the afternoon of 16 February an explosion was followed by a blast of flames shooting through the pit shafts. Timber and rock fell, blocking the way into the mine and hampering the rescue efforts. Above the pit a crowd of wives and children gathered for news and off-duty miners waited to volunteer to help with the rescue. It was known there were about 200 men working below ground, eventually three survivors, the first of the few who survived,

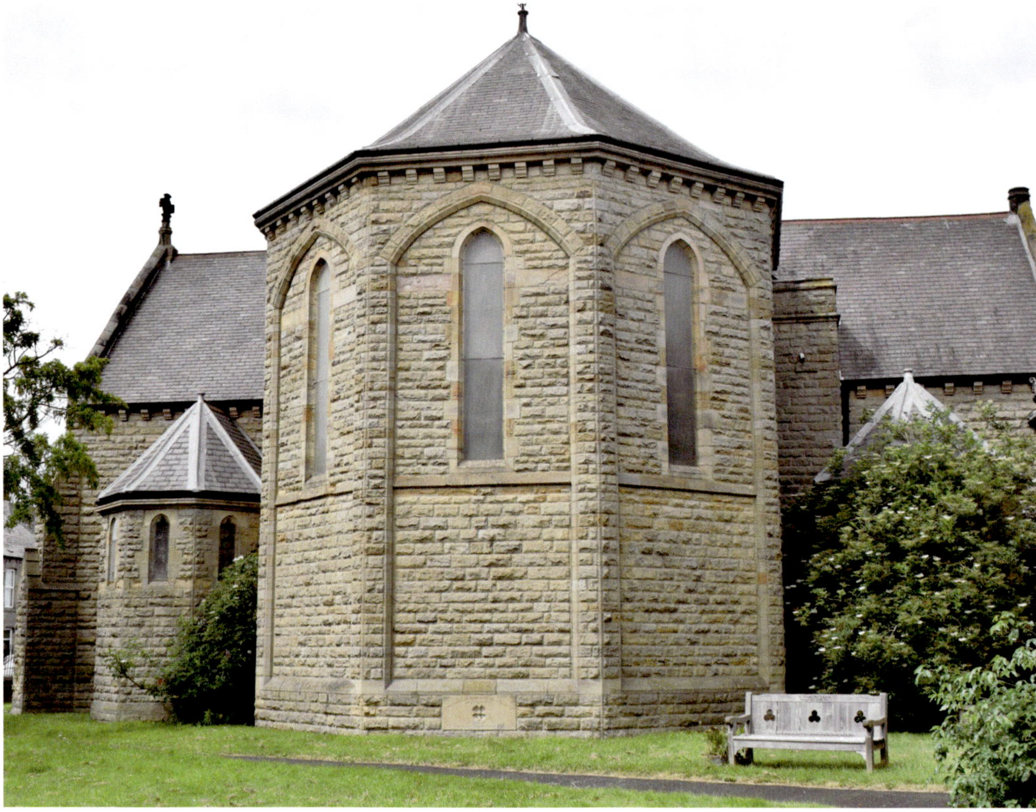

Above: St Joseph, Stanley.

Below: Many of those killed in the Stanley pit disaster were buried in mass graves. A memorial has now been erected to remember all those lost.

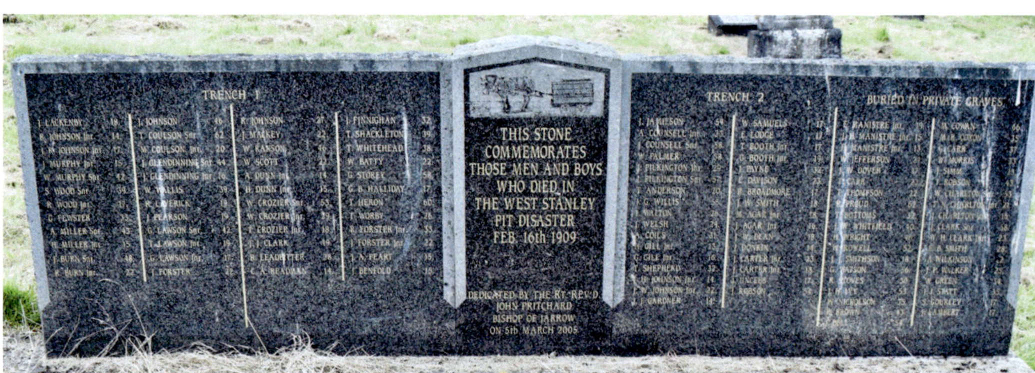

were brought out. Later 168 bodies were recovered. Burials took place in mass graves in St Andrew and St Joseph churches. Tragedy was felt in every street in the village and a relief fund was set up to help widows. Some were reported to be left with ten children to face an uncertain future. There were many teenagers

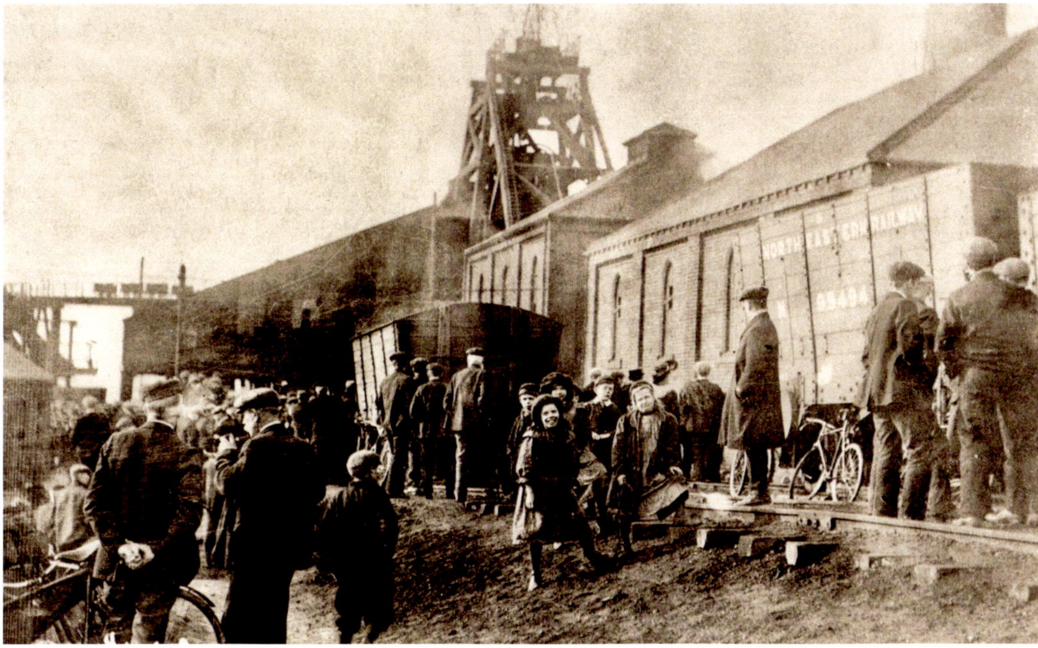

The 1909 disaster at Stanley brought many to the mine to await news.

killed in the disaster, the youngest of which was thirteen-year-old Henry Gill, whose parents also had to hear that his brother George, who was only three years older, had also died. There were two younger Gill children who would later follow their brothers into the mines – how the parents must have hoped for some alternative future for these boys.

46. Parish Church, Stockton-on-Tees

The church at the northern end of Stockton's wide High Street was opened in 1712. This was followed by the creation of a new parish, which separated Stockton from the ancient parish centred around the church of St Mary in the village of Norton a few miles to the north. Before this new church was built Stockton folk did have the benefit of a chapel of ease (a provision for the ease and comfort of those living a distance from the parish church). However, by the turn of the eighteenth century the vicar, Reverend Judd, described it as 'ruinous and too small and the ... inhabitants grow numerous'. Stockton was developing with merchants attracted to the port and market. The busy port had ships bringing timber and other building materials, tobacco and even coal to the port and leaving with lead from mines in Swaledale and grain from local farms. There was a thriving market where trading ranged from agricultural produce to livestock. A grand new church was needed for this prospering town. The design was influenced by Christopher Wren's architecture. Like Holy Trinity in Sunderland, which was completed in 1727, it is in a classic style, built around a main block. The design is much plainer than the Gothic styles that dominated church architecture from around 1200 to the Reformation. Gone are the

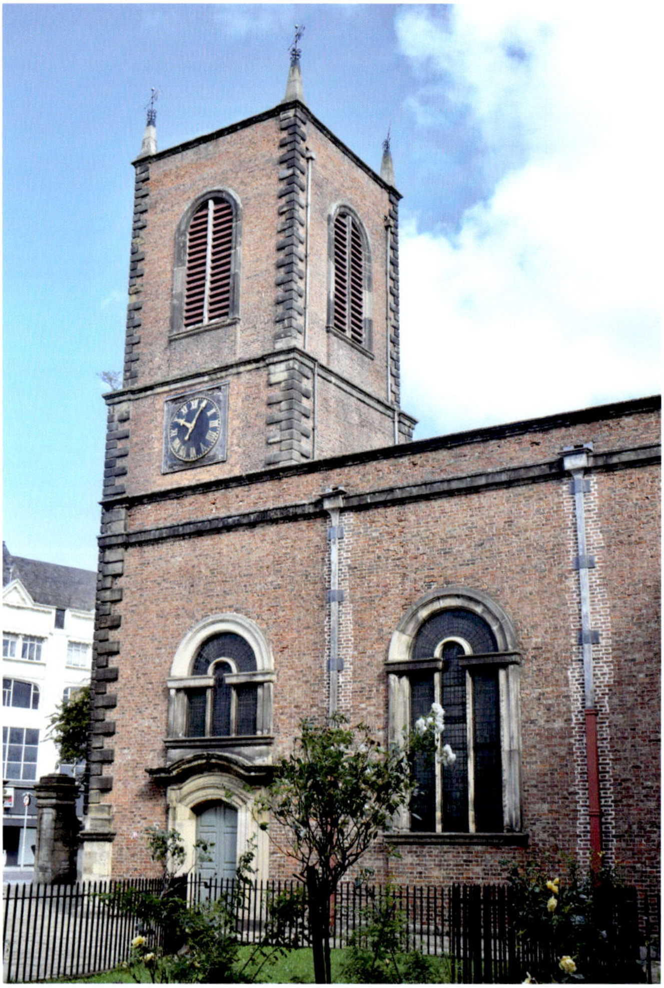

Parish church, Stockton-on-Tees.

decorated pointed windows and arches and vaulted ceilings that characterised the Gothic designs.

47. St Mary, Stockton-on-Tees

Gothic architecture was revived during the nineteenth century. This had much to do with the writing and designs of Augustus Pugin. His books *Contrasts* and *The True Principles of Pointed or Christian Architecture* looked back to the era before the Reformation and to the grand monasteries and churches that had provided, as he saw it, the only genuine Christian architecture. This was the time when the monasteries were places that provided aid for the poor, unlike during the nineteenth when the unfortunate were forced into workhouses. A step towards the old values could at least be taken in church architecture. He designed many churches and buildings, and perhaps amongst his most recognised work was in cooperation with Charles Bell on the Houses of Parliament in the 1840s.

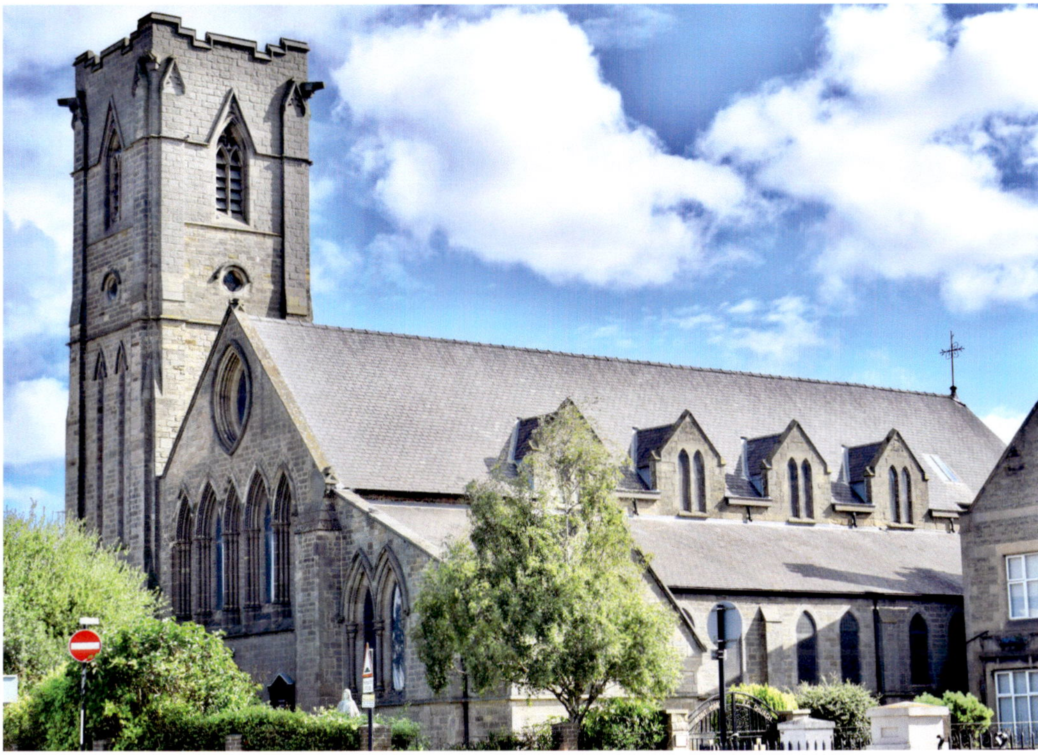

St Mary, Stockton-on-Tees.

Pugin's work is seen throughout the country, and he designed St Mary's Roman Catholic in Stockton. Reports of the opening of the church in July 1842 noted it was built 'under the superintendence of the celebrated Mr. Pugin' and told of an elegant church well placed on the road between Stockton and Norton with two schools, one for boys and the other for the girls. Later the tower and aisles were added, and the schools replaced. Pugin's son continued in his father's footsteps, working in the area at Crook and the Catholic Our Lady Immaculate and St Cuthbert Church.

48. Minster Church of St Michael and All Angels and St Benedict Biscop, Sunderland (formerly St Michael and All Angels)

This was once the church serving Bishopwearmouth, the parish on the south side of the River Wear in Sunderland. Little remains of early church; only parts of the chancel date to the fourteenth century, and the rest is from rebuilding in the nineteenth and extension during the twentieth centuries. In the early nineteenth century it was recognised that the parish was providing one of the richest livings in England, which attracted influential and distinguished rectors including Reverend G. Wellesley, the brother of the Duke of Wellington. The reverend became the centre of some controversy in 1831 when a report told that he was returning to the rectory after fifteen months away 'during which period he will have received £4,000 from Bishopwearmouth'. This highlighted one problem that was facing the established church: plurality, where clergy were awarded livings in a number of parishes, leaving the curates trying to cope with running the parish. Wellesley was reported to have roles at St Luke's in Chelsea, as vicar of Thetford, and as chaplain of Hampton Court and St James's. The *Durham Chronicle* thundered 'how long are the revenues of the church to be lavishly squandered upon men who appear to be made for this world only'. Legislation to limit the number of parishes that could be held was introduced in 1838 by the Pluralities Act, which restricted the number of benefices to two and they had to be within 10 miles of each other. The substantial income at Bishopwearmouth was eventually released and redistributed amongst the incumbents of the new churches built in the growing town. During the latter part of the eighteenth century Sunderland benefited from the ever-increasing shipment of coal from the docks. The next century brought rapid expansion of the town, again driven by coal, which was by then beginning to be carried by railway. A manufacturing base developed with shipbuilding, marine engineering, glass, paper, sawmills and forges.

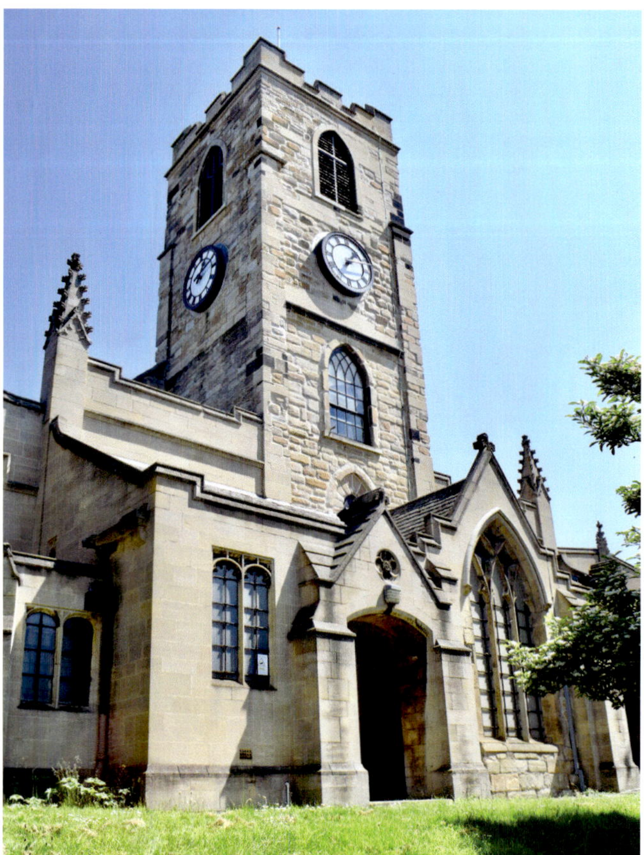

Minster Church of St Michael and All Angels and St Benedict Biscop, Sunderland.

Sunderland, being one of the largest towns in the county, with a population sufficiently diverse, attracted Nonconformist groups to add to the rich religious life. As well as becoming established in the west of the county, Baptists were in the town during the seventeenth century, as were a group of Quakers. A group of Presbyterians were in the town by the mid-seventeenth century and Congregationalists in the next century. These two groups merged in 1976 to form the United Reform Church. John Wesley was often in the town and indeed in 1774 'preached to the largest crowd ever in Sunderland'. In 1773 he was gratified by the acceptance of his work in Sunderland when, after preaching, he wrote 'surely God will be glorified in this place'. There was a significant Methodists presence throughout the town, with Primitive, Wesleyan, New Connexion and United Methodists all present.

49. St Andrew, Roker, Sunderland

At the start of the twentieth century Roker was an expanding suburb of Sunderland but was lacking a church. This was corrected in 1907 when the magnificent St Andrew's Church was opened, although at one time it looked as though a church might not be built. An appeal for funds had been made with limited success. Fortunately John Priestman came to the rescue and donated £6,000. John, from a

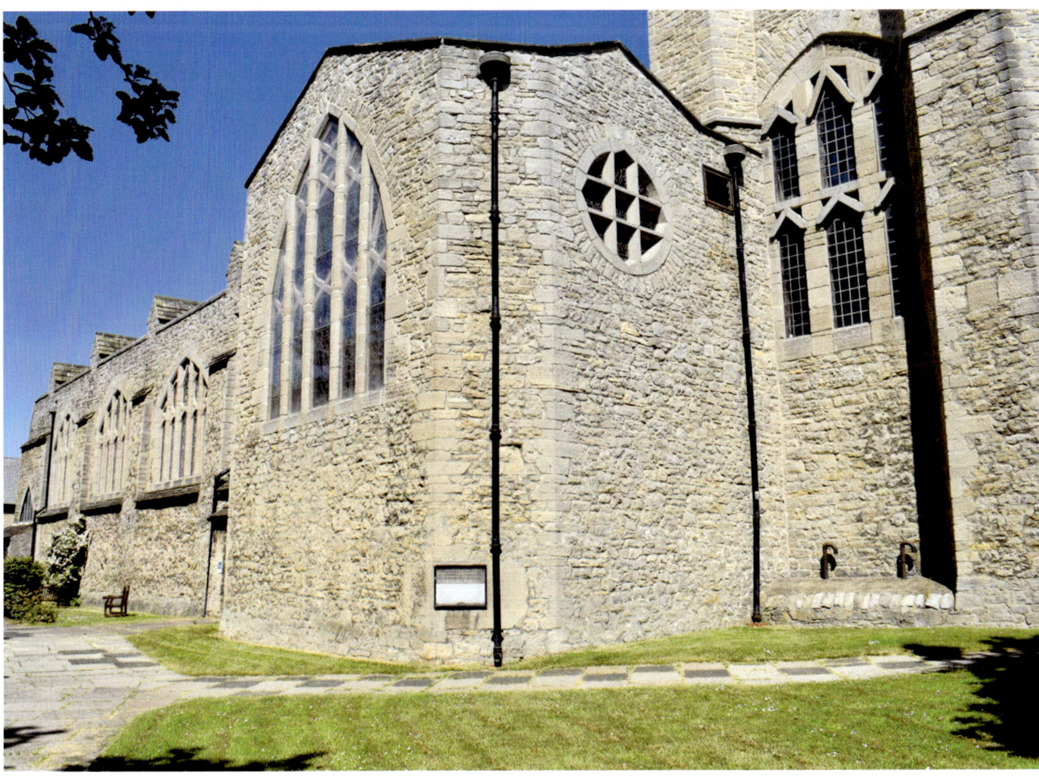

The patterns decorating the windows of St Andrew, Roker, in Sunderland, hint that this is no ordinary church.

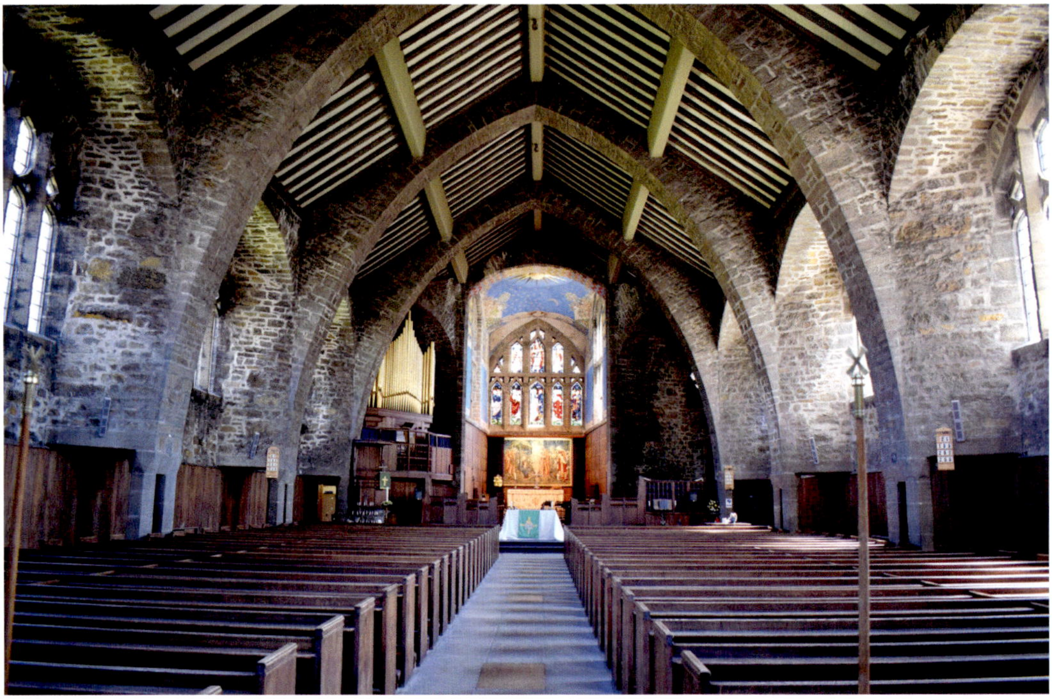

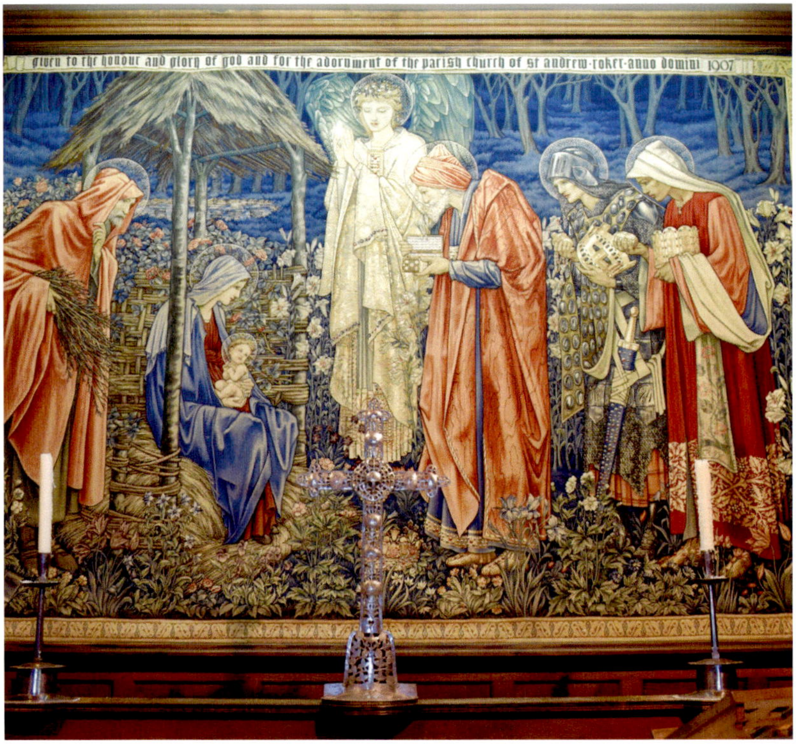

Above: St Andrew, Roker, described as the magnificent 'Arts and Crafts Cathedral'.

Left: In St Andrew's Church a tapestry depicting a nativity scene and the visit of the three wise men.

humble beginning as an apprentice for a Sunderland ship builder, went on to make his fortune in his own shipyard. This was not the only cause he helped; in the 1930s he gave £33,000 to pay for the renovation of the town's St Michael's Church.

This new church for the developing suburb has been described as the cathedral of the Arts and Crafts movement. Approaching St Andrew's, it has the look of a church but moving closer the decoration of the windows suggests there is something memorably different to be seen inside. It was designed by Edward Prior, who did much to establish the Arts and Crafts movement, a reaction against industrialisation and the ugly landscape that had been allowed to develop in towns and cities. His design moved from the traditional church design, construction and materials. Modern materials and building methods were used; inside there are no aisles and the vast arches span across the church giving uninterrupted views of the chancel. Stone masonry covers the arches to conceal the reinforced concrete used to form them.

50. St Boste, Oxclose, Washington

The Oxclose district of Washington is one of the villages that make up the town and is on what was once the site of a colliery. The hexagonal church was built in 1982 and is dedicated to a Catholic martyr, John Boste. He was born in 1544, became a teacher, then, after converting to the Catholic faith,

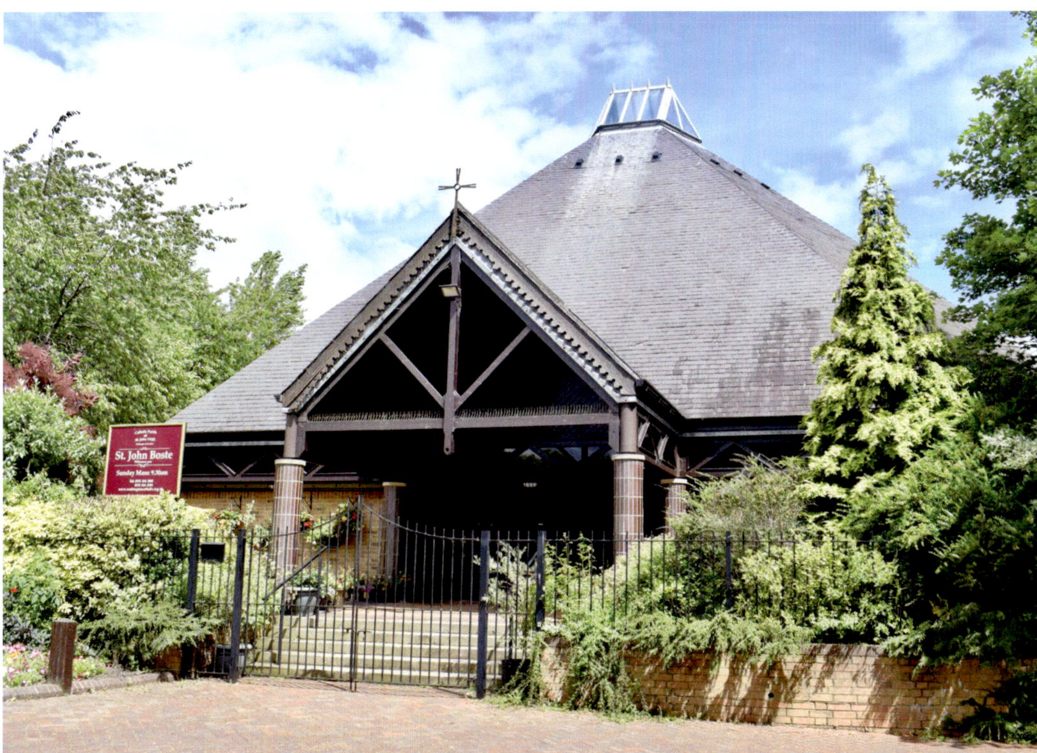

The late twentieth-century St Boste, Oxclose, Washington.

travelled to a British college at Rheims to train as a priest. This was during the time when Catholics were seen as potential traitors who threatened the stability of the country. Therefore, when his training was completed, he had to be smuggled back into the country. This was through Hartlepool in 1581 and from there he began life as a priest and became connected to a world of intrigue, spies, plots and informers. As he preached around the country, he sent reports of his work back to France. However, there was a spy working in France who in turn reported back to England. Elizabeth I had a network of informers built up to guard against plots by Catholic forces to overthrow her. Mary Queen of Scots also had to be watched as she posed a credible threat to Elizabeth. Mary had been implicated in the Northern Rebellion and was being confined in a castle in Staffordshire. Those watching her uncovered a plot to assassinate Elizabeth and assist Mary to take the crown. This was the Babington plot, led by Sir Anthony Babington. One of his fellow conspirators was John Ballard, who had been at Rheims the same time as Boste. It seems that Boste had helped Ballard by carrying letters to be shipped from Newcastle to their Scottish supporters. The plot failed – Elizabeth's spies in Mary's household intercepted letters to Andrew Babington. Ballard and Babington were executed along with other conspirators. Boste evaded arrest and was able to carry on his work until, whilst celebrating mass at a house near Durham, he was caught. Somebody had betrayed him. The Queen demanded he be taken to Windsor Castle, which was done secretly to prevent any rescue attempt, and from there he was taken to the Tower of London for interrogation and torture. He was sent back to Durham to face trial where he admitted 'I am a priest of the Holy Catholic Church and I came ... to reach the holy gospel of Jesus Christ'. This was taken as a confession, and he was taken by cart to Dryburn for execution in 1594.

51. Whitworth Church, Whitworth, Spennymoor

Unusually this church has no dedication. It was built in 1808 to replace a medieval church and major renovation followed in 1850. It is near Whitworth Hall, which came into the hands of the Shafto family in the seventeenth century and passed down through the family to Robert Shafto (1732–97). He served as Member of Parliament for Durham between 1760 and 1768. The hall was not too far from Brancepeth Castle where Bridget Bellasis lived, and the story goes that she became infatuated with Bobby and her hopes were recorded in the nursery rhyme.

> Bobby Shafto's gone to sea,
> Silver buckles at his knee;
> He'll come back and marry me,
> Bonny Bobby Shafto!

Unfortunately, this was not to be. Bobby became engaged to Anne Duncombe, heir to the Duncombe estate in North Yorkshire. The news of the impending marriage left Bridget so distressed that she died of a broken heart.

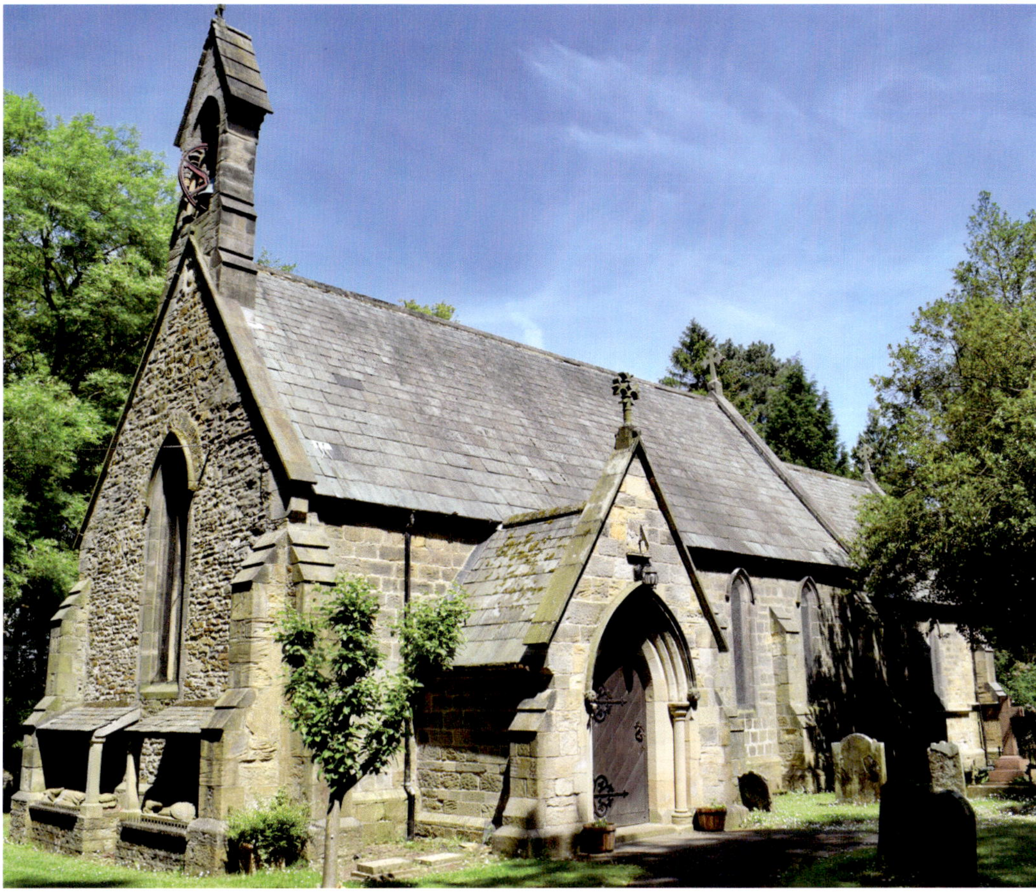

Whitworth Church. Under the canopies are medieval carvings of a knight and a lady.

Acknowledgements

'It will be a pleasure to show you around our lovely church' was the response from one lady when I contacted the parish office to ask if I could arrange a visit. This is only one example of the help I received from so many people that are not only so willing to guide and inform visitors but also give their time to looking after our churches. I must also record my gratitude for their help and to the church officials and the Parochial Church Councils for permission to use images including church interiors at Aycliffe, Brancepeth, Darlington, Escomb, Gainford, Edmundbyers, Heighington, Pittington, Stanhope, Sedgefield, Staindrop. Sunderland, South Church, Durham and Jarrow. The picture of the disaster at Stanley on page 87, the Sockburn Falchion on page 80 and the Jarrow marchers on page 54 are courtesy of the Beamish Museum People's Collection. The Sockburn church picture on page 80 is by Ataffo – Own work, CC BY-SA 4.0, https://commons.wikimedia.org/w/index.php?curid=72601566.